HEALTH TOURISM AND AYURVEDA

HEALTH TOURISM AND AYURVEDA

Robinet Jacob

ABHIJEET PUBLICATIONS
DELHI 110094

ABHIJEET PUBLICATIONS
2/46 Tukhmeerpur Extension
Delhi 110094
Phones: 011-22960492, 65698474
e-mail: abhijeetpublication@gmail.com
abhijeet_singh1@indiatimes.com

HEALTH TOURISM AND AYURVEDA

First Published 2008

ISBN 978-81-89886-33-2

Price: Rs. 580/- (INR)

PRINTED IN INDIA

Published by J.K. Singh fo Abhijeet Publications, Delhi 110094, Lasertypeset by Gaurav Graphics, Delhi and Printed as Himanshu Printers, Delhi.

Preface

Tourism is one of the most successful and fast growing business activities in the world. Economic diversification and technological improvement has created a very conducive environment for tourism development in the present age of globalization. Tourism industry acts as the backbone of many countries. It acts as a driving force for employment generation, poverty alleviation and social harmony.

Tourism is a multidimensional activity. The success of travel and tourism activity depends upon the success of a number of other sectors. Tourists are travelling with various purposes like leisure and recreation, business and professional journeys. Other tourism purposes are study, rejuvenation etc. India is a country with immense tourism resources. Diversification and enrichment of the existing resources will help the country immensely. A remarkable trend in the tourism activities is the growth and popularity of health care holidays based on Ayurveda.

Ineffectiveness of modern medicinal practices has forced people to think in favour of indigenous medicinal systems

and alternative lifestyles. The philosophy of *Ayurveda* takes a holistic view of health, emphasizing a balanced diet; physical fitness, healthy life style, hygiene and body care for a disease-free, long and healthy life. It gives due importance to both preventive and curative aspects of a disease.

Ayurveda is one of the greatest gifts the sages of ancient India have offered to mankind and is accepted as the oldest scientific medicinal system. The South Indian state of Kerala has sensed the potential for health holidays based on its century's old medicinal system, Ayurveda. Holidaying for fitness has struck its roots in Kerala. Kerala's equable climate, natural abundance of forests with a wealth of herbs and medical plants are a key to the success of Ayurvedic treatments of Kerala. There is an experimental proof that thirty percent of tourists to Kerala are for health holidays. This will help real estate, hospitality, transport and food & beverage industries. Ayurvedic tourism development has helped skilled, semi-skilled and non-skilled people in gaining employment.

This book is an effort to assess the present state of health tourism in Kerala based on Ayurvedic therapy. It examines various types of Kerala's unique Ayurvedic treatment methods. The study also tries to examine the existing Ayurvedic treatment facilities for tourists and their requirements. The state of tourism marketing activities and the impact of Ayurvedic tourism on the society and economy are also a part of the study.

The study on the whole is divided into six chapters. These chapters' deal with various aspects related to Ayurvedic tourism. The introductory chapter deals with, Health Management on an International and Indian Perspective, preconditions for healthy living, Medical Tourism etc. The second chapter deals with history, growth, basic principles and therapeutic approach to Ayurveda. The chapter also deals with the prime position of Kerala in Ayurvedic treatment. The third chapter focuses on the

relationship between Ayurveda and tourism in Kerala by explaining its Ayurvedic potential and the present state of tourism in the state. The fourth chapter deals with the availability of human resources, physical facilities and proper treatment methods. The fifth and sixth chapters deal with the impacts of Ayurvedic tourism on the society and economy. It also focuses on the present tourism marketing activities and its impact on Ayurvedic tourism in Kerala.

I would like to express my sincere gratitude to Dr.S.C. Bagri, Professor & Head, Centre for Mountain Tourism and Hospitality Studies, HNB Garhwal University who consistently provided me invaluable insight and suggestions and whose able guidance helped me in completing this work. I would also like to thank my dear friends and colleagues who have been a source of continuous encouragement and inspiration in the completion of this book.

Dr. Robinet Jacob

Contents

1

Ayurveda and Tourism

1.1 Introduction

Tourism is one of the world's most rapidly growing industries. Tourism related businesses are the leading producers of new jobs worldwide. It is a unique activity in which floating and migratory populations play a central role in the successful conduct of its various projects. The very term *"tourism"* is defined in the *Webster's Dictionary* as the "journey from place to place for excursion and sightseeing purposes". It means that in order to qualify an activity, as "tourism", people have to move from place to place individually or in groups, and enjoy the special sights and leisure offered by those places. The word 'tourism' or 'tourist' is related to the word 'tour' which is derived from the Latin word *'tornus'*. In French literature, the French term *'grand tour'* i.e., 'great tour' is used in the sense of tour through France, Germany, Switzerland and Italy. Hunziker and Krapt (1942) defined tourism as "the sum of the phenomena and relationship arising from the travel and stay of non-residents, in so far as they do not

lead to permanent residence and are not connected to any earning activity"[1].This definition distinguished tourism from migration and made the assumption that both travel and stay are necessary for tourism. World Tourism Organisation devised the following definition for tourism: "Tourism comprises the activities of persons travelling to and staying in places outside their usual environment for not more than one consecutive year for leisure, business or other purposes"[2]. A basic distinction among tourists can be made between domestic and international tourists. Tourists can also be classified by the purpose of visits too. This includes tourists travelling for leisure and recreation, business and professional journeys and other tourism purposes like study, health tourism etc[3].

A notable trend in global tourism has been the popularity of health care holidays. The tourism industry in India has been responsive and is making effort to cater to this ever-growing market based on Ayurvedic therapy. Health tourism based on Ayurvedic therapy is in the sphere of segmented and selective tourism and has become a craze among a particular section of tourists[4]. Its potential has become obvious and both the trade and tourism promotion authorities in liaison with those in charge of the indigenous system of medicine are evolving some norms for dispensing this therapy so that, it leads to diversification and enrichment of the tourism product.

Health holidays based on Ayurvedic therapy is popular in the south Indian state of Kerala. Public and private sector operators are in the field of offering Ayurvedic therapy to the fitness enthusiasts in the form of packages. Kerala has a fairly ancient Ayurvedic medical system, which is a treasure house of knowledge about natural medicine. Kerala has sensed the potential for fitness holiday packages and is trying to tap this market.

The philosophy of *Ayurveda* takes a holistic view of health, emphasizing a balanced diet; physical fitness, healthy life style, hygiene and body care for a disease-free,

long and healthy life[5]. The speciality of Ayurvedic treatment of Kerala is that it prolongs the span of life as well as refreshes and rejuvenates the vital organs of the human body. *Ayurveda* focuses on therapeutic and rejuvenate aspects[6].

1.2 Scope of the Study

Tourism is a constantly growing industry and has considerable potential in Kerala. The physical quality of life in Kerala is comparable to developed nations. A balanced climate, green vegetation, natural tourist spots, fully literate population etc. can be considered as Kerala's strengths along with world class health care systems including Ayurveda[7].

The significance of *Ayurveda* in tourism promotion of Kerala is of immense potential in view of health seekers and old age people's tourism market. This book is an attempt to bring about the basic issues involved in the field of Ayurvedic tourism development with special reference to Kerala. An effort is made to assess the present state of health tourism in Kerala based on Ayurvedic therapy. It examines the various types of Kerala's unique Ayurvedic treatment methods. This book intends to examine the existing Ayurvedic treatment facilities for tourists and their requirements. The state of tourism marketing activities and the impact of Ayurvedic tourism on the society and economy are also a part of this book. The results derived from this study could be used for careful planning and development of Ayurvedic tourism in Kerala.

Tourism activity is a relatively new development, and has been considered worthy of an academic study only recently. Tourism industry has sufficient economic importance and its impacts on economies, environment and society are serious topics requiring detailed research. Tourism consists of diverse industrial sectors and academic subjects. So an interdisciplinary approach is required for

conducting tourism studies. Tourism suffers from less availability of data sources in terms of both comparability and quality. The issues involved in this book include, social, economic, and cultural and matters related to marketing.

The study on the whole is divided into six chapters. The introductory chapter deals with the scope of the problem in general. The second chapter named "*Ayurveda* as a system of medicine" deals with the history and growth and the basic principles and therapeutic approach of *Ayurveda*. It also deals with the prime position of Kerala in Ayurvedic treatment. The chapter also analyses the various indigenous medicinal systems of the world. The third chapter "*Ayurveda* as a catalyst for tourism development in Kerala" focuses on the relationship between *Ayurveda* and tourism in Kerala. It also deals with the Ayurvedic potential and the present state of tourism industry in Kerala. An attempt has been made to discover the unique Ayurvedic products of Kerala in the fourth chapter named "Ayurvedic Tourism Resources and Facilities in Kerala". The focus of the study here is to analyse the availability of human resources, physical facilities and proper treatment methods. The fifth chapter named "Ayurvedic Tourism: Socio Economic Impacts and the Importance of Marketing" mainly deals with the impacts of Ayurvedic tourism on the society and economy. This chapter also focuses on the present tourism marketing activities and its impact on Ayurvedic tourism in Kerala. The concluding chapter deals with major findings and suggestions.

1.3 Health Management: An Indian Perspective

The technological changes which have occurred in modern medical treatment are amazing. It has helped humanity in a big way. At the same time, modern medicine has not been able to give a permanent solution to many diseases. It often goes for symptomatic treatment which is suppressive and even dangerous. Suppression of diseases

for instant relief may result in dreaded diseases. Health care systems in many parts of the world are in turmoil due to its mechanical and materialistic approach to health.

Violations of natural laws, stressful jobs, excessive eating, lack of exercise, drinking etc. are the causes of disease. A disease is most often the culmination of continuous unhealthy living habits. A holistic approach to health, giving prime importance to promotion of health rather than healing of diseases is the need of the hour.

Ineffectiveness of modern medicinal practices has forced people to think in favour of indigenous medicinal systems and alternative lifestyles. The success of indigenous medicinal systems like *Ayurveda, Homoeopathy, Unani, Siddha* etc. lies in its holistic approach and the importance it gives to enhance one's immunity or resistance against diseases. It gives due importance to both preventive and curative aspects of a disease. It emphasizes on a healthy living.

Indian villages were once known for their traditional treatment methods. Vedas, Upanishads and *Puranas* carried the message of healthy living which involves righteousness in thoughts, emotions and actions. *Ayurveda* enlightens us with an understanding of body constitution of a person, highlighting the necessity of personal participation and adaptation to seasonal changes, dietary intake, preventive measures and therapeutics. *Ayurveda* is not a structure or organ-oriented science. It is having a holistic approach to health. It considers a person as a compound of many aspects. Each person comprises of (1) body or *sharira,* (2) sense organs or *indriya,* (3) mind or *manas* and (4) self or *atma*. Healthy dietary alternatives, stress alleviating and body purifying massages and medicinal regimen help individuals to have a bliss of life. According to the constitution of World Health Organization (WHO), "health is a state of complete physical, mental and social well-being and not merely the absence of disease or infirmity". Mahatma Gandhi always reminded people of the value of health and he himself pursued a disciplined life in pursuit of health.

1.4 Preconditions for Healthy Living

- Vegetarian diet
- Moderation in eating
- Good combination of food
- Healthy food habits
- Abstention from alcohol, tobacco etc
- Harmony with nature
- Physical exercise
- Strong digestive fire and proper elimination of waste
- Positive thinking
- Ability to forgive
- Cleanliness of body and soul
- Maintenance of peace of mind through meditation, prayer and yoga

The emphasis on maintaining good health *(Swasthavartta)* is crucial to Ayurveda. The daily routine or *dinacharya,* and the seasonal regimen or *ritucharya* are designed to keep us healthy. In *dinacharya,* diet, physical exercise, personal hygiene and mental health are all important. Ayurveda being the science of life addresses every aspect of our lives, by incorporating the daily prescriptions for good health (of the mind, body and spirit) into our routines. The daily routine as advocated in Ayurvedic classics can be summarized as follows:

- Early rising, i.e. before sunrise *(Brahama muhurta)*
- Cleanliness
- Exercise depending on age and body constitution
- Satisfying natural urges in time
- Mental and moral discipline

1.5 Health Management and Tourism: An International Viewpoint

Pleasure travel for health was not available to the masses before the eighteenth century. This was due to lack of money and poor transportation facilities. Pleasure travel was considered as the privilege of the rich. The concept of health resorts and public baths can be traced to the Romans. The ancient baths introduced in the second century B.C, helped people to enhance health and social interaction. Baths were located by mineral springs or *Spas*. A *spa* or mineral spring is a place where people go to rejuvenate their body and mind. It is believed to have restorative powers.The medicinal properties of mineral springs gave origin to the *spa*. Health seekers find rejuvenation from it, either by drinking the water or by immersing in it. The need for additional facilities in the spa further caused the development of these spas into resorts with added facilities for pleasure and entertainment to their medical amenities.

In ancient Greece, patients used to come to *Epidarus*, where the shrine of *Asklepios*, the God of healing was located. They associated mineral springs with the gods and built holy wells and altars on the sites. The establishment of many sanatoria in Switzerland was a result of increased awareness about health among the local people.

In A.D. 1326, Colin le Loup, a Belgian citizen, was cured of a long term illness by the iron–rich waters of a spring near Liege.[8] In gratitude, he developed a resort there to welcome others which was renamed *Spa*, meaning fountain. The water of Tunbridge Wells in England was promoted as an aphrodisiac. Similarly, bathing in and even drinking salt water was considered as a cure for numerous diseases and helped promote seaside resorts. During the 18th century, rich Europeans used to visit health resorts in North Africa. By the year 1865, there were major seaside resorts in Italy, France, Britain and other Central European countries.

In the United States, seaside resort hotels were

established around spas in the eighteenth century in places like New York, Virginia and West Virginia. America's first resort city was the Atlantic City, developed in the late 1800s. It catered to those seeking the health benefits of sunshine and fresh air. The resorts and spas offered facilities for good food and gambling too.

Table 1.1

Staffing a Spa

- Massage therapists who can perform different types of massages and some body treatments.
- Cosmetologists who can style hair and perform manicures, pedicures and make up.
- Aestheticians who can perform facials, depilatory waxing and makeup.
- Fitness employees, who can teach classes, do one-on-one personal training, conduct fitness evaluations and coordinate certain recreational activities.
- Spa assistants or attendants, who can supervise the locker room, maintain cleanliness and perform some body treatments.
- Front-desk people who can meet and greet guests, act as concierges, and schedule all guest services.

Source: Monteson, Patricia A. & Singer Judith (1992). *The Cornell Hotel and Restaurant Administration Quarterly.*

1.6. Medical Tourism

The exorbitant cost of medical treatment in certain countries has given shape to a form of tourism activity called medical tourism. It can be broadly defined as provision of 'cost effective' private medical care in collaboration with the tourism industry for patient's surgical and other forms of specialized treatment. India is emerging as a prominent medical tourist destination. India's strength lies in its

different medicinal systems and its internationally competent health care professionals, holistic medicinal services and cost-effective treatments. India is blessed with a unique blend of various indigenous medicinal systems like *Ayurveda, Siddha, Unani, Homoeopathy* etc and western system of medicine i.e., *Allopathy*.

India is emerging as an important medical tourist destination. Most of the western patients are from countries where treatment is expensive and waiting lists are a routine. Most of them are in search of procedures that are not generally covered by health insurance like cosmetic surgery and hip resurfacing. India has gained acceptance in the areas of medical care such as assisted reproduction, bone marrow transplant, cardiac care, knee replacement, open-heart surgery, dental procedures, kidney transplant, neuro surgery etc. While a bone marrow transplant costs $26,000in India, it costs $2,50,000 in USA. A heart surgery costs $30,000 in USA, while it costs $6,000 in India. Along with the cost effective treatments, the clinical results achieved by Indian doctors are on par with the world's best hospitals.

A study conducted by the Confederation of Indian Industry (CII) and Mckinsey Consultants says that in 2005, around 1,50,000 foreigners visited India for medical treatment. The number is rising by 25 percent a year. India earned an amount to the tune of US$ 33.30 crores during the year. The study also says that India has the potential to attract one million medical tourists per annum by 2010 and this could contribute around U.S. $5 billion to the Indian economy. Medical tourists to India are from U.S.A., U.K., West Asia, Africa and South Asia.

The backbone of India's health care system is the English-speaking doctors, nurses and paramedical staff. The reputation enjoyed by the Indian medical professionals will help India's economy too. The institutions that cater to the foreign patients are situated mainly in New Delhi, Chennai, Bangalore, Mumbai, Hyderabad, Coimbatore, Kochi and Thiruvananthapuram. Some of the Indian

hospitals have secured certification from bodies like the Joint Commission International (JCI), a non-governmental agency of the United States of America that accredits hospitals as per American standards.

Medical tourism will supplement the tourism and hospitality industries too. The patients who come for treatment can use tourist resorts and destinations to recoup. The Apollo Hospital Group has made arrangements with the *Taj* group for transferring patients to its 38 leisure hotels. The emerging area of medical tourism will result in the quick growth of India's travel, tourism, hospitality and ancillary industries.

References

1. Holloway, Christopher J. (2002); *The Business of Tourism*, Pearson Education Ltd, Harlow, p. 2.
2. *Ibid.*, p. 3.
3. Chris Cooper, John Fletcher, David Guilbert, Stephen Wanhill (1994); *"Tourism – Principles and Practice"*, Pitman Publishing, London, p. 6.
4. *Promote Health Holidays*, (1998); Express Travel and Tourism, Mumbai, February 16.
5. Murthy, N. A. and Pandey, D.P. (1982); *Ayurvedic Cure for Common Diseases*, Orient Paperbacks, New Delhi, p. 15.
6. *Kerala: A Unique Destination where the season never ends* (1998); Express Travel and Tourism, Mumbai, June 8.
7. *The Kerala Companion*--Publication of the Department of Tourism, Kerala, p. 1.
8. Mill, R.C. (2001); *Resorts: Management and Operation*, John Wiley & Sons, New York.

2

Ayurveda as a System of Medicine

2.1 Indigenous Medicine

Man has evolved several methods for curing illness ever since the rise of human history. Different civilizations and societies have looked for different ways of curing diseases and thus gave shape to their own medicinal systems, which reflected their social beliefs, practices and way of life. Virtually every civilization has a system of indigenous medicine. The World Health Organisation (WHO) sponsored meeting at Brozzaville in 1976 has defined traditional medicine as "the sum total of all knowledge and practices, whether explicable or not, used in diagnosis, prevention and elimination of physical, mental or social imbalance and relying exclusively on practical experience and observations handed down from generation to generation, verbally or in writing".[1]

2.2 Various Medicinal Systems and Ayurveda

The need for curing diseases has resulted in the development of medicinal systems like *Ayurveda, Siddha* etc. in India, Chinese medicine in China, Greek medicine in Greece and *Unani* in Middle East. Due to the influence of the medicinal systems like *Unani, Siddha* and *Ayurveda* among the general public, Indian government has considered them as indigenous medicinal systems.

Many scholars consider *Ayurveda* as much older to *Siddha* and *Unani. Siddha* is considered as the Tamil version of *Ayurveda. Siddha* was preserved by the Dravidian race and legend has it that Lord *Muruga,* son of Lord Shiva in Hindu mythology, related the medical wisdom to sage *Agasthya* who in turn spread it among his disciples. The *Siddha* has its trace of origin beyond 10,000 years. There is not much difference between *Ayurveda* and *Siddha* in theory and practice. In *Ayurveda,* the medicines are mainly based on herbal plants and oils. But *Siddha* encompasses all the natural substances known to man for deriving medical remedies for diseases. The methodology of preparing medicines is such that it can change every matter into medicine with the proper configuration of components, through *vattu, oottu* and *neettu* i.e., distillation, sedimentation and reaction. *The Caliphs of Baghdad developed Unani during the eighth century A.D.* when Sanskrit and Greek medical works were translated into Arabic under the patronage of Caliphs Harun Al Rashid and Al Mansur. *Ayurveda, Unani* and *Siddha* are fundamentally similar in their approach to health and disease[2]. Indigenous medicinal systems are based on full of real experiences, observations and it is a combination of inspiration, intuition, facts and results.

Ayurvedic thoughts had a deep impact on the day-to-day life of the people of India. Almost everyone is aware of the treatments needed for common ailments. Ayurvedic principles of healthy living are widely followed by the Indian people. *Ayurveda* is the knowledge of healthy living

and is not restricted only to treatment of illness. The place of *Ayurveda* on the world map of healthcare is presently insignificant.

The healthcare system called "allopathic" or Western medicine was originated in the technologically advanced European Countries. *Ayurveda* suffered a great setback in India during colonial rule when they introduced western medicine. According to Swamy, (2001) "As every aspect of traditional culture, arts and crafts suffered during the two centuries of colonial exploitation, the Indian systems of *Ayurveda* and *Siddha* suffered a terrible blow. Western medicine has to its credit, a contemporary scientific approach as well as economic and political patronage" [3]. Allopathic medicines often give rapid cure and the treatment is based on symptoms. Sometimes these remedies may produce effects different from those of the disease. The differences between *Ayurveda* and western medicine are[4]:

- *Ayurveda* is essentially an experiential science in contrast to western medicine, which is an experimental science.
- *Ayurveda* has a holistic approach in contrast to western medicine, which is analytical in its approach.
- *Ayurveda* is a function oriented (Physiological) science in contrast to modern medicine, which is structure or organ oriented. Western medicine does not believe in function unless it is identified to be related to a structure, while *Ayurveda* looks at the whole organism as a total indivisible being which has to function as a whole to exist as a whole.

Ayurveda is full of observations and conclusions without the support of scientific experimentation. The ancient scientists have unfolded the secrets of nature by substantiated hypothesis, which they proved as a result of examination and re-examination for a number of

centuries. According to *Charaka samhita* "there is very little that can be obtained from direct proof. The province beyond, direct experimental evidence is vast"[5]. This can be understood only by the method of inference. The manner in which *Ayurveda* analyses the functioning of the human body is fundamentally different from the parameters of modern anatomy and physiology. *Tridosha (vata, pitta, kapha)* classification in *Ayurveda* is dominantly important in understanding human physiology. As per this system the entire treatment and methods are related to these classifications, which find no parallel in western medicine. Nodal points of acupuncture in the Chinese systems cannot be explained from the perspectives of modern anatomy. Similarly *Ayurveda* too has to be recognized as yet another medicinal system in which ancient India has understood the functioning mechanism of the human body. Each of these forms of different medicine is successful in its own way. Unlike allopathic and most other systems of medicine where treatment follows the curative method, *Ayurveda* follows the preventive method. In taking a preventive medicine approach to treatment, a lot of importance is given to life styles of the people.

2.3 Origin and Growth of Ayurveda

Ayurveda is one of the great gifts of the sages of ancient India to mankind and is accepted as the oldest scientific medicinal system, with a long record of clinical experience. *Ayurveda* can be called "The science of living". It traces its etymology to *Ayu,* meaning 'life' and *Veda,* which means 'knowledge'. *Charaka* has defined it as the science through which one can obtain knowledge about the useful and harmful types of life, the span of life as well as the very nature of life. According to Indian mythology, *Ayurveda* was first perceived (not composed) by *Brahma* and he taught this science to *Daksha Prajapati* who, in turn, passed it to *Ashwinikumara* twins who were the physicians to gods. The *Ashwinikumaras* then proffered this knowledge to Lord *Indra.* This story is practically constant in several texts[6].

According to *Sushrutha Samhita, Lord Dhanwantari* and his disciples learnt it from Lord *Indra*. But according to *Charaka Samhita, Bharadvaja* and *Atreya* learnt it from Lord *Indra* and they passed it over to their disciples. As per *Brahma Vaivarta Purana, Bhaskara* composed *Ayurveda* as the fifth *veda* on the advise of *Prajapati* which was handed over to his 16 followers. They in turn wrote so many books. According to *Kashyapa Samhita, Kashyapa, Vasishta* etc. learnt *Ayurveda* from *Lord Indra*.

References to the Ayurvedic principles of medicine are found in most of the Vedas. There are four Vedas named *Rig, Yajur, Sama* and *Atharva veda* which have come down to us through several thousands of years of oral transmission before finally being recorded in writing. Vedas are regarded as the oldest scripts or records of knowledge known to man. They are stated to be of divine origin and given to mankind through the *Rishis* and there after transmitted from generation to generation. Even though references to the various principles of medicine are found in most of the Vedas, the main body of *Ayurveda* is found in the fourth *Veda*—the *Atharva veda*. However even though *Ayurveda* is part of the *Atharva veda*, it is also recognized as an *Upa* or supplementary Veda in its own right.

2.4. The Phases of Ayurvedic Development

The period of the origin of *Ayurveda* is considered to be around 6000 B.C. The exact period of its origin is in the mists of antiquity. All legends are of the opinion that *Ayurveda* was given shape by Brahma. The legends can be considered as a part and parcel of the pre-Vedic period, about which nothing is known on factual basis.

During the Vedic period, the four Vedas—*Rig Veda, Sama Veda, Yajurveda* and *Atharva Veda* were formulated. The general essence of teaching of Indian philosophy is explained in these texts. It consists of religious hymns and has references to certain medical principles. These four

Vedas constitute the four pillars of the ancient Indian philosophy. The fourth Veda, the *Atharva Veda* gives details of the state of medical knowledge during the Vedic period. The *Ayurveda* science is an *upanga* (supplement) veda[7]. The eight branches of *Ayurveda* are mentioned in *Atharvaveda*. But the knowledge about the basic principles of *Ayurveda* was not documented during this period.

The growth and development of *Ayurveda* occurred mainly during the *Arsha* period - the period of rishis. This period extends over several centuries. *Dhanwanthari* and *Bharadwaja* learnt the principles of *Ayurveda* from *Lord Indra* and developed the surgical and medical systems around 9th century B.C. During those days, a teacher's instructions were recorded by his students and then transmitted orally to their disciples. A number of treatises on *Ayurveda* were written during this period. The six disciples of *Atreya,* who developed the school of medicine namely *Agnivesha, Bhela, Jatukarna, Parashara, Harita* and *Ksharapani,* wrote the *Shatbhishak samhita. Agnivesha samhita* was also written during this period, which was revised by *Charaka.* It is considered as the oldest medical book existing.

Similarly the school of surgeons under *Aupadhenava, Vaitarana, Aurabhra, Pushkalavata, Gopurarakshita* and *Sushruta* developed *Shalya tantra* (Surgery). *Sushrutha* was the first surgeon who developed systematic and exhaustive ways of operative techniques to deal with various problems of the human body. *Sushruta Samhita* written by him is considered as an authentic book on *Shalya tantra.*

In ancient India, *Ayurveda* was practiced as a system of medicine. During the period of Lord Buddha and afterwards while Buddhism was finding its way to the other parts of the world, *Ayurveda,* also made inroads into these countries and became a global system of medicine. In the ancient days, *Ayurveda* was imparted through the *Gurukula* system of education. Successful students were allowed to practice only after obtaining a certificate issued by the ruler of the land. This ensured that *Ayurveda* was never misused,

and it always passed into right hands. A lot of Ayurvedic research also took place during this period in India.

Ayurveda suffered a setback under the onslaught of the British colonial rulers. The British perceived it as a threat and tried to destroy it by legalizing its practice by anyone who chose to do it. This led to the mushrooming of dubious Ayurvedic practitioners all over the country and to a serious damage to the credibility of *Ayurveda* among the common people. This stayed for centuries till long after the British colonialists had left India. *Ayurveda* is on the path of revival as a result of the initiatives taken by the central and state governments. Various state governments started Ayurvedic colleges and set up examination boards to conduct Ayurvedic examinations. The central and state governments have appointed drug controllers and drug inspectors for quality control. Now the governments are spending substantial percentage of their health budget to provide Ayurvedic aid to the public. Post independence, the central and state governments took several measures to revive *Ayurveda* and now there are 14252 dispensaries, 2189 hospitals, 187 undergraduate and 51-post graduate teaching institutions in India. Health policies have accorded *Ayurveda* the same status as *allopathy* in India. The chronological development of *Ayurveda* is shown in figure 2.1.

2.5. Ayurvedic Literature and Studies

Different exponents of *Ayurveda* wrote a large number of treatises on *Ayurveda*. Although they differ in certain instructions, the basic principles remain the same. These *Samhitas* (compendia) of *Ayurveda* are written in Sanskrit, the language of ancient India. The ancient original *samhitas* used the non-Paninian form of Sanskrit. They are not prepared based on the grammatical rules laid down by *Panini* who formally wrote the grammar of Sanskrit for the first time. The use of non-Paninian form of Sanskrit makes interpretation of *samhitas* very difficult. For easily

Fig.2:1
Representation of chronological development of *Ayurveda*

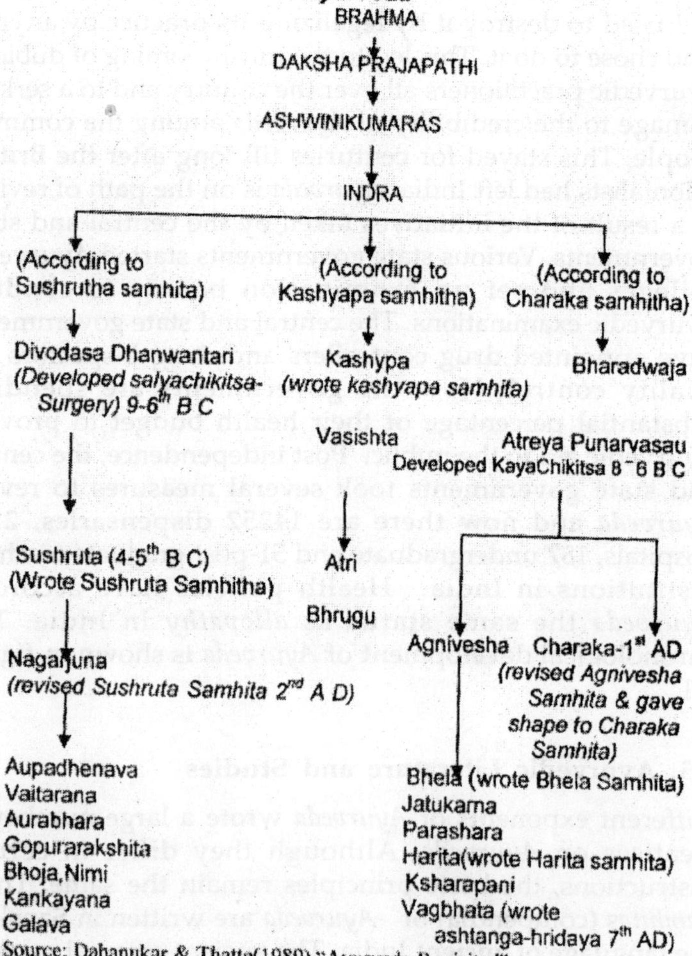

Source: Dahanukar & Thatte(1989) "Ayurveda Revisited"
Modified page 13

propagating *Samhitas,* they were written in the form of *sutra* (Stanza)[8], which made it precise. It was easy to memorize but unfortunately subjected to different interpretations. Thus the *samhitas* underwent considerable additions, omissions, modifications and editorial revisions from time to time. The growth of *Ayurveda* was made systematic due to the existence of two great universities in India, which taught various subjects along with *Ayurveda* in detail. One was *Kashi* where Sushruta headed the medical section. The other one was at *Taxila,* where medicine was taught by *Atreya* and later by *Charaka.*

2.6. Branches of Ayurveda

According to *Charaka Samhita* and *Sushruta Samhita,* it was Lord Brahma who composed *Ayurveda* and divided it into eight branches since he believed that man had limited life and intelligence[9]. The branches of Ayurveda[10] are

➢ *Kayachikitsa:-* (General Medicine)

Kayachikitsa means the treatment of diseases pertaining to *Kaya* (body). It deals with the ailments of adults not treated by other branches of *Ayurveda.* Hence it is known as general medicine.

➢ *Balachikitsa :-* (Paediatrics and Gynaecology)

This branch deals with the prenatal and postnatal baby care as well as the care of women before and during pregnancy. It also elaborates various diseases of children and their treatments.

➢ *Grahachikitsa: -* (Psychiatry)

This branch deals with mental diseases and their diagnosis and treatments. Treatment methods include not only medicines and diet but also yogic methods for improving psychic power.

- *Salakya Chikitsa:-* (ENT and Cephalic Diseases)

This branch deals with diagnosis and cure of diseases of ear, nose, throat, mouth and eyes.

- *Salya Chikitsa:-* (Surgery)

Maharishi Sushrutha is the first surgeon who introduced *Salyachikitsa,* the foremost specialty of *Ayurveda.* He describes various surgical operations using different surgical instruments and devices.

- *Agada tantra:-* (Toxicology)

This branch deals with the diagnosis and treatment of toxins from vegetables, minerals and also toxins from animal origins. The concept of pollution of air and water in certain places and seasons has been given special consideration. Such pollution is also said to be the cause of various epidemics.

- *Rasayana Tantra* (Gerontology or science of Rejuvenation)

This branch deals with prevention of diseases and promotion of long and healthy life. It also advises how to increase our health, intellect and beauty along with capability of alleviating diseases.

- *Vajikarana Tantra:-* (Aphrodisiac treatment)

This branch deals with the means of enhancing sexual vitality and efficiency.

Besides these eight branches, *Ayurveda* also deals with diseases affecting plants and animals. They are *Vrukshayurveda*, which deals with the diseases and treatments of plants, and *Mrugayurveda,* which deals with diseases and treatments of animals.

2.7. The Contents of Ayurveda of Samhitas (Compendia)

The *Ayurvedic Samhitas* (compendia) are divided into sections. Each section deals with different aspects of *Ayurveda* giving instructions for preservation of health, cure of diseases and maintenance of long life in a state of happiness. The *Samhitas* are divided mainly into sections. Each section is called a *Sthana*. Each *Sthana* is even subdivided into chapters too.

The various sections of *Charaka Samhita* is as follows.[11]

- *Sutrasthana:-* it deals with origin, general principles and philosophy of *Ayurveda*.
- *Nidanasthana:-* it deals with causes of diseases.
- *Vimanasthana :-* it deals with factors affecting drug administration.
- *Sharirasthana:-* it deals with anatomy and embryology.
- *Indriyasthana:-* it deals with diagnosis and prognosis.
- *Chikitsasthana:-* it deals with treatment of diseases.
- *Siddhisthana:-* it deals with the cure of diseases.
- *Kalphasthana:-* it deals with Pharmacy.
- *Uttarasthana :-* it deals with diseases and treatments which are not mentioned in other *sthanas*.

The contents of the chapters are summarized at the end of the chapter and then at the end of each section. Generally there are 120 chapters in the major *samhitas*. The concept that the duration of human life is till 120 years is the basis of this method. But *Vaghbhata's Ashtanga Samgraha* consists of 150 chapters. Certain *Samhitas* lacked certain *Sthanas* as they gave importance to medical principles narrated in other *sthanas*. *Sushrutha samhita* is one such example. It lacks the sections *Indriyasthana* and *Vimanasthana* as it deals in greater detail with *Sharirasthana*.

2.7.1. Prominent Samhitas

The teachings of *Atreya* were collected and his disciple *Agnivesha* prepared a Samhita. *Agnivesha Samhita* was well accepted and was propagated as the backbone of Ayurvedic Science. It contains 46,500 verses. Later *Charaka* revised it in the 1st century A.D and he gave shape to *Charaka Samhita*. In the 3rd or 4th century A.D. it was again revised by *Dhrudabala* by making certain additions. *Charaka Samhita* gives much importance to *Kayachikitsa*.

Around 4-5th century B.C., Sushruta, the disciple of Dhanwantari, wrote Sushruta Samhita. It gives much importance to *Salyachikitsa*. *Sushruta* developed major surgical principles. Later during 2nd century A.D., *Nagarjuna* revised it. Another prominent *Samhita* is *Kashyapa Samhita*, which was written by *Kashyapa*. It is considered to be written during the Gupta period. *Bhela, a contemporary of Atreya, wrote Bhela Samhita.*

Vagbhata wrote *Ashtanga Hridaya* and *Ashtanga Samgraha*. *Ashtanga Hridaya* is not an independent treatise, but it is an edited compilation of the best from *Charaka Samhita* and *Sushruta Samhita*. So it gives details of *Kayachikitsa* and *Salyachikitsa*. According to Dr. P.C. Ray, *Vagbhata's* period was before A.D. 800. *Harita, a disciple of Atreya,* wrote *Harita Samhita*.

In 1890, Bover, a British military officer retrieved seven old books from Kashgar in Central Asia. Out of the seven books, three were all about *Ayurveda*. It is known as *Navneethakam* or *Bover's* manuscripts.

Vagbhata compiled his two treatises from the two former authors, *Charaka* and *Sushruta*. This was when chemistry was making its presence felt in the treatment of diseases in the form of mercury. *Charaka* and *Sushruta* heavily relied on plant products and herbal medicines. *Samhitas* like *Rasaratna Samuchaya*, *Rasaratnakara* or *Rasendramangala* were based on the therapeutic effects of mercury. The *Sharangadhara Samhita* written by

Sharangadhara was influenced by *Unani* system, as it was prepared during the 13th century A.D. The 14th century publication, *Ayurvedaprakasha* by *Madhava* gives details of the therapeutic use of gold in preparing medicines. This also shows the influence of *Unani* on *Ayurveda* system. The compendia on *Ayurveda* after *Vaghbata's Ashtangahridaya* like *Madhvanidana, Vrindamadhava, Chikitsasara Samgraha, Kaumarabhrutya, Rasaratnakara* etc were ancient, but it is of a relatively recent period.

The introduction of more therapeutic measures other than herbal medicines led to the formation of *Nighantus* (lexicons), which gives details of drugs. The oldest among them is the *Dhanwantari Nighantu*. There are twelve *Nighantus,* which gives the names and properties of various drugs.

There are medical systems, which developed out of Ayurveda or were influenced by it. One such system is the Tibetan system of medicine[12], which is the main stay of the majority of the Tibetan people. *Ayurvedic Samhitas* were translated into Tibetan, from Tibetan to Mongolian and further into other languages of Central Asia and to Greek. Indian medical works of *Charaka* and *Sushruta* were translated into Arabic language under the patronage of Caliph Al Mansur. Western medicine, till the 7th century A.D. was based upon the Latin version of this Arabian translation. The medical treatises in *Simhala* language of Sri Lanka were prepared based on the ancient Sanskrit *Ayurvedic Samhitas*. Thus *Ayurveda,* the Indian indigenous medicinal system made a remarkable development in India as well as influenced contemporary medical systems of other societies. Historical incidents in the development of *Ayurveda* are shown in table 2.1.

Table 2.1

Historic Events in the Development of *Ayurveda*

Period: (A.D.)	*Ayurvedic works*
100	Revision of *Agnivesha Samhita by Charaka*
200	Revision of *Sushruta Samhita* by *Nagarjuna.*
400	Translation of Ayurvedic texts into Chinese.
700	*Vagbhata* wrote *Ashtangahridaya* and *Ashtangasamgraha.*
800	*Madhavacharya* wrote *Madhava Nidhana*
900	*Vrindamadhava* wrote *Siddhayoga* or *Vrindamadhava*
1100	*Chikitsa Samgraha* and *Dravyagunasamgraha* written by Chakrapanidatta.
1200	*Chikitsasarasamgraha* written by *Vangasena.* Compilation of the principles of the schools of *Charaka* and *Sushruta.*
1300	*Dhanvantari Nighantu*-Beginning of the inclusion of mercury in therapeutics.
1381	*Veerasimhavalokana*- written by Veerasimha, the king of Gwalior.
1400	*Sharangadhara Samhita*- Sharangadhara
	Kaurnarabhrutya-Prithvimalla
	Rasendrasarasamgraha-Gopalakrishna
	Rasendrachintamani-Dhundukantha
1500	*Rasaratnakara*-Nityanatha
	Rasakoumudi-Madhava.

1600	*Bhavaprakasha*-Bhava Mishsra.
	Raja Todarmal wrote *Todalananda* or *Ayurvedasoukya*
1666-68	*Yogasamgraha, Yogachintamani, Vaidyachikitsa Samgraha* by Harshakeertisuri mentions for the first time, *Phirangaroga,* the sexually transmitted disease.
1700	*Yogaratnakara*
	Chikitsaratnavali-Kavichandra.
	Ayurveda Prakasha-Madhava Upadhyaya.
1800	*Gadanigraha*-Sodalan
	Bhaishajaratnavali-Govindadasa (Included therapies for diseases of kidney and brain)
	Vaidyamrita-Narayana
1800-1830	*Vaidyakashabdasindhu*-First Ayurvedic dictionary in Sanskrit by *Umeshchandra Gupta.*
1870-1910	Efforts for translation of Ayurvedic books to Vernacular languages.
	Ayurvedic magazine in Bengali:-*Ganga Prasad* Sen.
	Pratyakshasareeram-Gananatha Sen.
	Translation of *Charakasamhita* in Marathi-Shankar Daji Shastri.
	Ashtanga Sareeram and Brihatsareeram by P.S. Warrier.
	Opening up of Kottakal Arya Vaidyasala at Kottakal near Calicut by *P.S Warrier.*

Source: Compiled by author.

2.8. Development of Ayurveda in Kerala

Kerala's Ayurvedic system is not fundamentally different from the main stream. The age-old texts act as the leading force of Kerala's Ayurvedic system. Kerala's Ayurvedic methodology mainly follows *Ashtangahridaya* and *Ashtangasamgraha* wrote by *Vaghbata*. *Ayurveda* became popular in Kerala with the arrival of Sanskrit in Kerala. Certain traditional treatment methods were believed to be followed in Kerala before the arrival of Sanskrit. So the history of *Ayurveda* in Kerala can be divided into three phases-Pre-Sanskrit arrival period, Post-Sanskrit arrival period and the Modern period.

2.8.1. Pre-Sanskrit arrival period- (Before 5th century A.D.)

During the ancient period, South India was known as *Chentamilnadu*. During those days, people belonging to different communities showed interest in medical systems. The famous literary work *'Tholkapium'* was published in the first century A.D. This book explains the six professions of Brahmins, but there is no mention of the *'Vaidya'* (medical) profession. But there is a mention on a particular community called *'Velas'* and a method called *'Veriyattu'* which is used for treating women.[13] *'Veriyattu'* is a treatment method combining magic and medicine. There is also a mention of the use of oil after delivery by women. This proves that medical profession was not the monopoly of any particular community. This also gives ample proof of the existence of a developed medical system in ancient Kerala.

2.8.2. Post-Sanskrit arrival period (After 5th century A.D.)

The influence of Sanskrit in Kerala started around A.D. 5th, 6th and 7th centuries. The *'Vaidyas'* (medical practitioners) of Kerala mainly used the two texts written during 5th century A.D. by *Vagbhata* for guidance. Sanskrit was studied by people belonged to every community. Brahmins and Namboothiris conducted rituals. Clashes were less

between members of different communities. This along with the mentality to accept all beliefs and practices resulted in forming a congenial atmosphere for all intellectual activities including *Ayurveda*. Although *Vagbhata* was a Buddhist, and the two texts of *Vagbhata* was influenced by Buddhism, the liberal mentality of the Brahmins of Kerala or the thought that Buddhism was not different from Hinduism encouraged the people to accept the medical principles in those texts in their daily life. *'Ashtavaidyans'*, a group of families who followed Ayurveda profession, led Ayurvedic movement in Kerala. There was a need for medical practitioners in the 18 villages of Brahmins. The families who were proficient in Ayurvedic medical system acted as *'Vaidyas'* to these villages and handed over their knowledge hereditarily. Along with *'Ashtavaidyans'* some other families and various communities like *Velas, Ganakas, Kurups, Ezhavas* etc also specialized in various areas of ayurvedic treatment. The Venetian traveller Marcopolo, who visited Kollam in Kerala in the 13th century A.D., has reported the "abundance of good doctors and astrologists".

2.8.3 Ayurvedic Literature of Kerala

The Ayurvedic Literature of Kerala can be classified into three[14].

- Commentaries of the basic *samhitas* (compendia) and independent books based on the content of the *samhitas*.
- Collections of various indigenous treatment methods used by *'Vaidyas'*.
- New books published in the modern period.

The prominent *Ayurvedic Samhitas* followed by the Keralites were *Ashtangahridaya* and *Ashtangasamgraha*. Numerous commentaries were written in Kerala based on these two *samhitas*. One among them is *'Sasilekha'* written by *Indu,* a Keralite and a disciple of *Vagbhata*. Other commentaries include *'Padhyam'*, *'Bruhal Padhyam'*, *'Kairali'*,

'Hrudya', *'Lalitha'*, etc. A book named *'Sahasrayogam'* which is commonly used in the state by the *'Vaidyas'* gives details of so many treatment methods which are not followed any where else. Books like *Rasavaiseshikam, Rasopanishad, Vaidyamanorama, Dharakalpam, Sindhura Manjari, Alathoor Manipravalam* etc. are considered as prominent Ayurvedic literary works which explains the specialties of Kerala's Ayurvedic treatment. During the Dutch rule in Kerala, an Ayurvedic lexicon named *'Hortus Indicus Malabaricus'* was prepared under the leadership of the Dutch Mayor Henry Van Reed. The information for this was received from a local medical practitioner named *Itti Achutan*. This gives us an idea about the quality of Ayurvedic knowledge Kerala inherited and developed. Important milestones in the development of *Ayurveda* in Kerala are shown in table 2.2.

Table 2:2

Important Milestones in the Development of Ayurveda in Kerala

Sl.No.	*Ayurveda Works*	*Author*
Commentaries based on *Ashtangahridaya* and *Ashtangasamgraha*		
1.	*Sasilekha*	Indu
2.	*Padhyam*	Unknown
3.	*Bruhalpadhyam*	Unknown
4.	*Hrudya*	Unknown
5.	*Lalitha*	Pulamanthol Mooss
6.	*Kairali*	Pulamanthol Mooss

Table 2.2 (A)

Books based on Ayurvedic Literary Works

Chikitsamanjari	Pulamanthol Mooss
Vakyadeepika	Parameshwaran Namboothiri
Saradarpanam and Bhavaprakasam	Kaikulangara Rama Warrier
Bhaskaram	Uppottu Kannan
Arunodayam	Govindan Vaidyar
Hrudaya Priya and *Sukhasadakam*	Pachu Moothathu
Yogamrutam and Ashtangasaram	Pachu Moothathu
Sarachandrika (A commentry on Madhavanidana)	Parur Kesavanasan

Table 2.2 (B)

Independent Books

Rasavaiseshikam	Bhadanta Nagarjunan
Rasopanishad	Unknown
Sindhooramanjari	Thaikkattu Narayan Mooss (1046-1083)
Alathoor Manipravalam	Alathoor Nambi
Sahasrayogam *Chikitsakramam* *Yogaratnaprakashika* *Vaidyamanjari* *Chikitsanool* *Sannipadachikitsa* *Netrarogachikitsa*	These books are followed in Kerala only- Authors unknown.
Vaidyamanjari	Puthukkattu Madathil Krishnanasan

Source: Compiled by author.

2.8.4. *Special Ayurvedic Methods of Kerala*

A number of treatment methods which cannot be seen in the basic Sanskrit Samhitas and *Ashtangahridhya* are followed in Kerala. These are available in a book named *'Sahasrayogam*. Certain Ayurvedic medicines like *'Gorochanadi'*, *'Kombanjadi'*, *Dhanwantaram'*, *'Kasthuryadi'*, etc. are used in Kerala only. *'Ilaneerkuzhambu,'* a medicine based on coconut is used against eye diseases. Coconut, coconut oil and other coconut products which are plenty in Kerala is an unavoidable part of Kerala's Ayurvedic medicines and *oils*. Glandular secretion of certain animals like Cevet are also used due to its medicinal properties, *Dhara, Pizhichil, Njavarakizhi, Thalam*[15], etc. and its numerous types are Kerala's traditional Ayurvedic treatment methods. These methods of treatment and healthy living are the contributions of Kerala to *Ayurveda*. Kerala has offered a lot to *Ayurveda* by introducing its own effective treatment methods and drugs in dealing with diseases related to *Vishachikitsa, Balachikitsa* and *Salakyachikitsa*.

2.8.5. *Modern period*

The early proponents of *Ayurveda* studied and taught this science in the *gurukula* system. So many organizations along with the government came up with efforts to start organized and structured studies in *Ayurveda*. In 1886, Kaviyoor Perameswaran Moothatu established an Ayurveda study centre at Thiruvananthapuram. Later in 1890, the then Travancore government took over the study centre and handed it over to the department of indigenous medicine. In 1918 it became a college conducting B.A.M.S. and M.D. courses. An eminent scholar *Vaidyaratnam* P.S. Warrier started *Aryavaidyasala* at Kottakkal near Calicut in 1902. It became one of the most famous Ayurvedic colleges in India.

2.8.6. *Modern Books*

The person who gave significant contributions to

Kerala's *Ayurveda* in the modern period is *Vaidyaratnam* P.S Warrier. He tried to reform Ayurvedic system and Ayurvedic education. He started the world famous *Aryavaidyasala* at Kottakkal. For effectively teaching *Ayurveda,* he wrote two books *Ashtanga Sareeram* and *Brihat Sareeram.* He published a magazine named *'Dhanwantari'* with the help of Sri. P.V. Krishnawarrier.

Other prominent modern books include *'Sareeram'* written by Dr. A.L. Ravivarma, *'Panchakarma'* written by Sri Manakkodan Keshavanvaidyar, *'Vasti pradeepam,* by *Panavalli Kartavu* etc. These modern books helped in refining *Ayurveda* and in making Ayurvedic principles and books acceptable and accessible to many people.

2.9. Basic Principles of Ayurveda

Ayurveda is the ancient Indian health science developed through research work conducted over the centuries by the *rishis* (sages), who were eminent scholars. *Ayurveda* is a compound of two words: *Ayu* which means 'life' and *'Veda'* which means knowledge. As the term *'Ayurveda'* denotes 'the knowledge of life', it is not only a system to cure disease but the system teaches us how to achieve perfect health from diseased or abnormal conditions and how to lead our life, both physical and mental and to attain the bliss of real life.

Ayurveda deems health as the perfect condition of a man having a happy combination of thought, action and speech. Revitalizing this healthy condition and making one vigorous and immune to diseases is one of the cardinal principles of *Ayurveda.* This is achieved through a perfect harmony with nature. Ayurveda advocates the prevention of disease rather then cure. The guiding motto of *Ayurveda* pharmacology is *'Jagathyeva Manaushadam'* meaning there is nothing without any medicinal value in the world. So *Ayurveda* uses every thing like trees, food grains etc. and metals like gold and silver. Certain animal products are also used.

Ayurveda is thousands of years old and still survives in today's sophisticated world due to various reasons. Its basic principles were derived from the universal laws of nature. It is based on principles and observations, which has been constantly re-examined for a number of centuries. *Ayurveda* relies on deep observation of nature's functioning to understand the physical and non-physical aspects of life. It points out the intimate relationship between the processes occurring in nature and those going on in human bodies. The pillars of *Ayurveda* lies on the principles like *Panchamahabhutas, Tridoshas, Prakruti,* effects of seasons, *Panchakarma* etc.

2.10. The Four Aspects of Life

Ayurveda is a complete philosophy of life. It gives equal important to the non-material components of human lives like mind thoughts, emotions and consciousness. *Ayurveda* considers *ayu* or life as the coordination of four parts of life: *atma* (soul), *manas* (mind), *Indriyas* (senses) and *sharira* (the body)[16]. *Ayurveda* focuses on maintaining a balance among them.

2.10.1. *Atma (The Soul)*

Atma is the motivating intelligence that guides the mind as well as all of life[17]. The ancients could identify its existence by the way people ascribe ownership to things. They found that *atma* or sense of 'I' directed all aspects of life. The ancients concluded that there was an unimaginable intelligence responsible for creating and coordinating the vast diversity of the universe. All the aspects of life acted in coordination with every other part for the greater good of the whole. This would only occur if every part was connected to that intelligence which had knowledge of the whole. The ancients deducted that this governing principle existed as a part of us, guiding all mental, sensory and physical processes. They identified *Jivaatma,* the quality of intelligence associated with the

individual consciousness within us. They also identified the universal quality of intelligence within us as *param atma* (universal soul), which is responsible for unifying all diversity. *Ayurveda* uses a term called *dharma* to explain the idea of the soul's special purpose and path. Each soul's inbuilt preferences lead it to make choices which are consistent with its *dharma*. People receive joy when they are doing things, which are closely related with their soul's purpose.

2.10.2. *Manas (The Mind)*

Ayurveda teaches that mind is ultimately responsible for maintaining the harmony between the parts of human life and the universal intelligence that coordinates all of life. All phenomena in the universe come under the influence of three phases of activity called the three gunas.[18] Nature is using its creative mode known as *sattva,* to bring life into manifestation. It then uses its activating phase called *rajas* to maintain what has been created. Later it uses its destructive mode called *tamas,* to bring it to an end. The influence of these *gunas* is universal. The same *gunas* exists in our minds too. *Sattva* gives us the ability to imagine, to think and to create. *Rajas* generate action and motivation while *tamas* in the mind offers us the ability to bring it to completion. Although human beings are basically the same, their reactions to events will differ depending up on the specific balance of *sattva, rajas* and *tamas* in our minds. Distortion of this balance occurs due to three reasons. The stimulus, which is generated by mind, which results in certain kind of thoughts and emotions, is the first reason. The stimulus, which is created due to types of things we chose to take in through the senses, is the second reason. The final source of stimuli is the body, influencing *manas* through what we eat and drink. Any stimulus whether mental, sensory or physical can have predominantly *sattvic, rajasic* or *tamasic* influence on the mind.

The *sattvic* mind always selects things that nourish growth and are aware of things that are beneficial for it. A *rajasic* mind has the knowledge of what is best, but it will often stay away from doing things and becomes unsteady. In *tamasic* nature, the mind forgets what is good for it, and becomes lost in thoughts and activities, which have negative effects. *Ayurveda* tries to eradicate *tamas* or ignorance, which surrounds the mind by eliminating toxic impurities which results in regaining the balance of mind.

2.10.3. *Indriya (The Senses)*

The *indriyas* connects the non-physical parts of life i.e. *atma* and *manas* with the physical body and environment[19]. The *indriyas* collects information from the outer world and transmits it to the mind in the form of sound, touch, temperature, light, colour, taste, flavour and smell. If the information gathered by the senses is of inappropriate quality and quantity, it will create imbalance in the mind, ultimately resulting in imbalance to the body. Excessive and insufficient use of senses can create imbalance in the mind. Sensory intake, which is morally or emotionally unacceptable, also, results in imbalance of mind. These types of misuse of senses will harm it and the co ordination between the body and the mind will be weakened. When compared to *rajasic* and *tamasic* mind, with a *sattvic* mind, the senses will act as exact receptors and accurate transmitters of information between the body and the mind. Thus *indriyas* act as a link between the outside world and our selves.

2.10.4. *Sharira (The Body)*

Sharira (The body), is the fourth fundamental part of the life. *Ayurveda* considers the body as the medium through which we can influence the non-physical components of life. *Ayurveda* gives equal importance to all the four fundamental parts of life. A healthy living can be ensured

by properly removing pollutants accumulated in the body. *Ayurveda* suggests this through *Panchakarma*.

2.11. Panchabhutas (The Five Element Theory)

The *Panchabhuta* theory states that universe is composed of five basic elements or *Panchabhutas*. The five elements are akash (space), *vayu* (air), *agni* (fire), *jala* (water), and *prithvi* (earth)[20]. Every thing in the universe, including the food and bodies we possess, is derived from these *bhutas*. A fundamental harmony therefore exists between the macrocosm (the universe) and the microcosm (the individual). Human beings are comparable to the cosmos being a miniscule image of it.

2.11.1. The Panchabhuta Theory and the Human Body

Ayurveda has observed that the same laws of nature that governs the elements *(Panchabhutas)* and their interactions in the world must necessarily govern the elements within our bodies[21]. Our bodies are structured after the food we eat, the water we drink, and the air we breathe. These things are the various combinations of the five elements.

2.12. Dosha, Dhatu and and Mala—The Three Components of the Body

Ayurveda gives us a comprehensive understanding of the physical substances that compose the body as well the organising intelligences that create and govern their functions. The *Panc..abhutas* or five elements are represented in the human body as *doshas, dhatus* and *malas*[22]. According to *Ayurveda,* the human body consists of these three fundamental components.

2.12.1. Dhatus and Their Functions

The *dhatus* are the body constituents that form the basic structure of the body, each one having its own function.

They exist in many forms: liquid, semisolid and solid. The *dhatus* are those substances and structures, which are retained by the body and are a part of body's composition and give it its physical strength and function. *Dhatus* are seven in number. Unnatural loss of *dhatus* could lead to death. The disequilibrium of the *dhatus* results in diseases and maintenance of equilibrium is considered as perfect health[23].

The following are the *dhatus*[24]

- *Rasa*—food juices
- *Rakta*—*haemoglobin* portion of the blood—Life force
- *Mamsa*—muscle tissue—cover bones
- *Meda*—fat tissues
- *Asthi*—bone tissue—Helps to stand and walk.
- *Majja*—Bone marrow—Nerve tissue nourishment.
- *Shukra*—Semen Reproduction.

2.12.2. *Malas and Their Functions*

Malas are bye-product of the *dhatus,* partly used by the body, and partly excreted as waste matter after the process of digestion is over. These play a supporting role while they are in the body, and when they are eliminated; their supporting role is finished. The useful elements are retained and absorbed by the body while the *malas* (waste matter) are excreted in the form of faecal matter, sweat, urine, mucus, tears, saliva and carbon dioxide. If the *malas* do not get excreted from the body at the appropriate time and in proper quantity, their accumulation causes an imbalance that damages the functioning of the *dhatus.*

The following are the three *malas*[25]

- *Puriksha* (faecal matter)—Removes toxins in solid form through the colon.

- *Mutra* (urine)—Removes toxins in liquid form through the kidney.
- *Sweda* (sweat)—Removes toxins through the pores of skin.

2.12.3. *Tridoshas*

The theory of three *doshas* is the crown jewel of Ayurvedic science and the cornerstone of all its diagnostic and treatment modalities. The three *doshas* are the primary and essential factors of the human body that govern our entire physical structure and function. *Ayurveda* considers *doshas* to be of vital importance, because it is responsible for co-ordinating and directing all the structures and substances of the body. There are three *doshas* in the body. They are *Vata, Pitta* and *Kapha*[26]. There are no direct equivalents for these three *doshas*, known as *tridoshas*. However the factors responsible for movement and sensation in the whole body are the representatives of *Vata*. The factor responsible for digestion, metabolism and energy are the representatives of *pitta*. The factors responsible for strengthening the stomach and the joints, providing firmness to the limbs, and refreshing the sense organs are the representatives of *kapha*. There are some special areas in the body in which each *dosha* predominates, namely, the chest for *kapha*, digestive organs for *pitta* and the large intestine for *vata*. Direct perception of three *doshas*, which do not exist on the physical plane is not possible; it is possible to discern their presence and influence by examining their effects on the organism. Bile, Phlegm and other bodily secretions are vehicles for the three *doshas*, substances through which they display their qualities and perform their actions.

Tridoshas are condensed from the *panchabhutas*. *Vata* arises from *akash* (space) and *Vayu* (air), *Pitta* from *agni* (fire) and *Jala* (water), and *Kapha* from *Jala* (water) and *prithvi* (earth). The three *doshas*, like the elements from which they arise, increase and decrease in the body

according to the qualities which we absorb from food, drink and our environment. Even our thoughts and emotions have qualities that affect the body's *doshas*. All five elements are essential to life and their harmony, which arises when *vata, pitta,* and *kapha* are balanced, determines an individual's condition or disease. A healthy organism produces just enough of the three *doshas* to meet physical needs, while an unhealthy body overproduces or under produces the *doshas* at the expense of the body's vitality, adaptability and community.

2.12.4. Tridoshas *and Health*

When any of the *doshas* becomes excessively agitated or increased disproportionately in relation to the others, an imbalance is created and disease results[27]. The balanced state of *doshas* is health. The loss of dynamic equilibrium may be due to the excessive or deficient use of or the misuse of the five sense organs- the ears, skin, eyes, tongue and the nose; action of body, mind or speech; and time (different seasons). The restoration of health would depend on regaining the balance among the *doshas*. The balance would depend on the consumption of environmental matter in right form, proportion, combination and at the right time. Environmental matter in the form of drug or a diet will correct the disequilibrium.

2.13. Body Constitution

The ancient teachers of *Ayurveda* made a classification of body constitutions or *deha-prakritis* based on the theory of *tridoshas*. The predominance of one *dosha* determines the constitution that a human being has. If there is an excess of *vata,* it results in a person having a *vatala* constitution. Similarly the dominance of *pitt*a gives rise to *pittala deha-prakriti* and *kapha* to *shleshmala dehaprkriti*. The other four constitutions depend on the vitiation of more that one *dosha*. In certain persons, the three *doshas* tend to go out of equilibrium altogether. The presence of all *doshas* in a

balanced state is good[28]. The *deha-prakritis* are pre-determined body constitutions that a person is born with and there is no change in their basic structure till one dies.

Each type of body constitution has some peculiar dietary and other habits, and a certain predictable response to drugs. Medicines cannot be prescribed for a patient until the physician has taken in to account the type of constitution of the patient. A drug, which helps one type of body constitution, will not help a person with a different body constitution. *Ayurveda* maintains that illness results from the disturbance of equilibrium among the three *doshas* and other body constituents[29]. Any loss of that balance in an individual makes him susceptible to various disorders.

2.14 Digestion and Health

Digestion plays a key role in Ayurveda's concept of human health and illness. *Ayurveda* teaches that all diseases originate first in mind, but on a physical level this comes out as a break down of metabolic function. *Ayurveda* confirms the importance of digestion to supply the nutrients, which enable each *dhatu* to perform its job. It also states the importance of proper elimination of by-products occurring from digestive process.

Ayurveda states that indigestion is both the inability to eradicate metabolic waste products that results from digestive process. Indigestion will result in so many disorders. The food which remains in the gastrointestinal tract in undigested form is called as 'Ama'[30]. If this toxic sticky residue is not quickly burned up by the digestive process, it will accumulate in the G-I tract. When *ama* becomes too plentiful in this area, it will be removed by the *doshas* and will be transported to the *dhatus*. It will result in the break down of co-ordination of the *doshas*. The natural *doshic* process of eliminating *malas* will be disturbed. Function of *dhatus* will also be hampered due to the destruction of its ability to assimilate food and

medicine. All these will ultimately result in causing diseases. So *Ayurveda* states the importance of proper digestion in maintaining health.

Ayurveda gives much emphasis on strong, efficient digestion because it is vital for connecting the parts of life to their basis in wholeness. Any breakdowns in the activities, which nourish one *dhatu* ultimately weaken the health of all the *dhatus*. When *ama* is already present in the body, *Panchakarma*, Ayurveda's science of rejuvenation, provides the primary means to rebuild health. Through its purification procedures, *Panchakarma* re-establishes balance among the *doshas*, normalises digestion and removes the toxic accumulations from the *dhatus*.

2.15. Ahara, Vihara and Aushadhi

Ayurveda considers the concepts of *ahara, vihara* and *aushadhi* as the basic pillars on which health, happiness and harmony with natural law rest[31]. *Ahara* and *vihara* are concerned with diet and life style and are basically preventive in nature. When the imbalance in the body cannot be handled by *ahara* and *vihara, aushadi,* the method of treating disease is used.

2.15.1. *Ahara*

Ahara means 'intake' and refers to knowledge of proper diet. Although diet will not cure long-established diseases, majority of illnesses can be controlled merely by adjustments in diet and eating habits. *Ahara* is concerned with the effects of the various types of food on the quality of mind, the digestion and the balance of the *doshas*. *Ayurveda* also recognises the significant role of proper nutrition in maintaining mental *sattva*.

2.15.2 *Vihara*

The principle of *vihara* or 'activity' explains how to act in ways that support life, and includes life style guidelines

to maintain optimum health and balance. The sophisticated and complicated lifestyle keeps our minds always active. The negative influences from our environment also create fear and confusion. Due to these reasons people are not able to experience the vast physical, mental, and emotional resources that are hidden in them. The effective way to enhance the quality of *sattva* is meditation. Taking rest is another way of promoting *sattva* in the mind. *Vihara* also advises us to do only reasonable work. Exercise stimulates muscle metabolism and increases oxygenation. Exercise will help people to become rejuvenated.

2.15.3. *Aushadhi—Ayurvedic Disease Management*

Ayurveda uses two distinct modalities in the treatment of disease each with its own purpose. *Shamana* therapy is the one used to handle the symptoms of disease, whereas *Shodhana* therapy is the one used to eradicate the cause of the disease which occurs due to increased doshas[32]. *Shamana* therapy, the procedures for alleviating the symptoms keeps the *doshas* at their place but gradually brings down their negative influences by the application of medicines. It makes the patient feel better by suppressing the effects of the body's accumulated *ama*. *Shamana* therapy is done where accumulation of imbalanced *doshas* is less in quantity. *Shodhana* therapy removes *ama* and *mala* from the body and restores the balances of the *doshas*. In this from of treatment, the basis of the disease process is eradicated. *Panchakarma* is the most important *Shodhana chikitsa* or purification therapy.

Major factors which results in diseases in the body

- Undigested food material *(ama)*
- Imbalance of *vata, pitta* and *kapha*
- Weak digestive fire
- Vitiation of the body tissues *(dhatus)* and the body wastes *(malas)*
- Vitiated state of body channels *(srotas)*

Fig 2:2

Method of Ayurvedic Disease Management

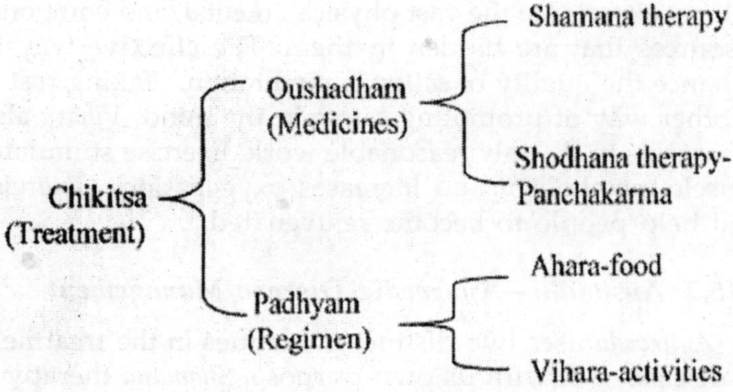

Source: Compiled by author

2.16. Panchakarma

Disease process is the result of accumulation of ama toxicity in the body. *Panchakarma* is the most important *shodhana chikitsa,* because it reverses all disease mechanisms, which carry *ama* from the digestive tract into the tissues of the body. *Panchakarma* is designed to take *ama* out of the *dhatus,* return it to the digestive tract and expel it from the body. The sanśkrit term *panchakarma* constitutes two words *pancha* (five) and Karmas (actions). It is the five procedures for purifying the body, mind and consciousness.

Panchakarma therapy is more than the five pacificatory and rejuvenative procedures. It is a three stage process, in which the *panchakarma* treatment serves as the focal point. Some measures need to be taken before and after the *panchakarma* therapy is applied. They are known as *Purvakarma* and *Paschatkarma*.

2.16.1. *Purvakarma and Paschatkarma*

Purvakarma is the preparatory procedure whose purpose is to prepare the body to discharge accumulated *ama*. This is undertaken before the actual *Panchakarma* therapy is administered. *Panchakarma* starts with purvakarmas which includes *deepana* and *pachana* (use of digestives and appetizers), *snehana* (oleation) and *swedana* karma (fomentation)[33]. *Snehana* refers to internal and external oleation. This saturates the body and helps to liquefy *ama* and other toxins in the body. In external oleation, medicated oils are vigorously massaged into the body. In internal oleation, medicated oils are ingested. Oily preparations given are ghee, oils and fats. *Swedana* karma is designed to induce sweating by therapeutic application of heat to the body. This process loosens the toxins and the process can be accelerated by the addition of herbal preparations to the steam. After a few (usually three to seven) days of *purvakarma* the *doshas* are ready to be flushed out of the system by one or more of the *Panchakarma* procedures. *Paschatkarma,* the final phase occurs after *purvakarma* and *panchakarma*. A variety of preparatory procedures can be used not only to enhance elimination and purification during *panchakarma* but to rejuvenate specific zones of the body. They generally employ some form of *snehana* or *swedana,* and often address the functions of a particular *dosha*. Such a variety of procedures which can also be used out side *panchakarma,* by themselves or in conjunction with various treatments are used at various parts of India including Kerala with local differences. *Paschatkarma* is a special post dietetic regimen, which is designed to restore the digestive and absorptive capacity of the person, thus restoring him to a normal state of health[34].

2.16.2. *Panchakarma Procedures*

The body normally uses three routes to eliminate waste products and toxins: the mouth, anus and pores of the skin. *Panchakarma,* the foremost purification therapy reverses

disease mechanisms by eliminating the toxic waste products and *ama* through these three routes of elimination[35]. *Panchakarma* programme slightly varies from school to school. Table 2:3 shows the five Karmas according to *Charaka Samhita* and *Sushruta Samhita*.

Table 2:3

Panchakarmas according to Charaka Samhita and Sushruta Samhita

According to *Charaka Samhitha*	According to *Sushruta Samhita*
● *Vamana Karma* (emesis)	● *Vamana Karma*
● *VirechanaKarma* (Purgation)	● *Virechana Karma*
● *Niruha Vasti* (non-oilyenema)	● *Vasti*
	● *Nasya or Sirovirechana*
● *Annuvasana* (oily enema)	● *Rakta Mokshana* (Blood-letting)
● *Nasya or Sirovirechana* (head evacuation)	

Source: Compiled by Author.

2.16.3. *The types of Panchakarmas*

1. *Vamana karma* (Emesis)

Vamanakarma is an important *pradhana karma* of the *Panchakarma* therapy. Literally, *vamana* means to expel the vitiated doshas through the oral route. This procedure is for discharging excess *kapha* and *kaphic ama*. *Vamana* is always preceded by suitable *purvakarmas* in order to mobilize the *doshas*. A variety of *vamana* drugs are used to induce it. The body naturally wants to eliminate the toxicity which impairs its functioning and *vamana* is a natural procedure to eliminate *kapha*-related impurities.

2. *Virechana karma* (Purgation)

Virechana karma is for expelling the *doshas* through the anal passage. *Virechana* is the specific therapy for *pitta dosha* disorders. *Virechana* expels *pitta* from the *amasaya* (stomach and upper part of the small intestine) which is not performed by *Niruhavasti,* though the latter uses the anal route for elimination. *Virechana* is a controlled process that gathers *ama* from many *pitta* locations in the body concentrates it in the small intestine and then discharges it. It purifies *pitta* function and consequently balances and strengthens all metabolic processes.

3. *Vasti karma* (Enema)

Vasti karma is the most powerful of the five main procedures of *panchakarmas.* The term *vasti* is derived from the fact that *vasti yantra* or the apparatus used for introducing medicated materials is made up of *vasti* or an animal's urinary bladder. The *vasti* procedure, applied through the anus may be *niruha vasti* or *annuvasana vasti. Vasti* is the introduction of medicated liquids into the colon through the rectum. When *vasti* is used in conjunction with *Panchakarma's* pre-procedures, it cleans the colon as well as purifies toxins from all over the body. It restores the balance of the *doshas. Vasti* is of two types; *niruhavasti,* which consists of the use of decoction of appropriate drugs and *annuvasana vasti,* which uses oily *substantces.* In certain cases a combination of both these types of *Vasti* is given.

4. *Nasya* or *Sirovirechana Karma* (Head Evacuation)

Nasya is a term applied for medicines or medicated oils administered through the nasal passage. *Nasya karma* is considered the best and the most specific procedure for diseases of the head. This procedure rejuvenates the tissues and organs of the head and neck. It introduces medicated oils and powders into the nose, the nearest access and outlet to the organ of the head. It removes *ama* from the head region. *Nasya karma* is said to prevent diseases of the eyes, ears and nose.

5. Raktamokshana:-(Blood-letting)

Sushruta gained a deep understanding of the relationship of the blood to *rakta dhatu, pitta dosha* and diseases associated with their toxicity and malfunction. He combined the two main types of *vasti* introduced by *Charaka* into one category and added *rakta mokshana* – the therapeutic withdrawal of blood from the body – as the fifth major procedure used in *pancha karama* therapy. *Sushruta* noted that when *ama* or toxins collected, they were circulated throughout the body with the blood. He devised *rakta mokshana* as a purification treatment to be used when excess toxins are being carried in the blood to various parts of the body. *Rakta mokshana* is the most limited among *panchakarmas*.

Pancha karma procedure offers the most effective treatment for cleansing the body and eliminating the root of the disease. They remove the substances, which weaken the body and break down health and restore life to a balance. *Panchakarma* represent the ultimate in *Shodhana chikitsa*. *Panchakarma* concludes with treatment designed to nourish and strengthen the body, called *paschatkarma*, or post procedures.

References

1. Dahanukar, Sharadini and Thatte, Urmila (2000); *Ayurveda Revisited*, Popular Prakashan, Bombay p. 1.
2. Tourism India, (June – July 2001); *Siddha Vaidhya, the Complete & Medical Principle*, Thiruvnanthapuram, p.7.
3. Swamy, Krishna Mohan (2001); *Reflections on Ayurveda*, the Hindu, Coimbatore, Sept 4.
4. Kurup, P.N.B. (2002); *Ayurveda, The Treasure of India*, Science India, Thriruvananthapuram, p. 50.
5. Charaka Su.11:7.
   Pratyaksham he alpam analpam apratyaksham asti yada agaman upamanayukti bhi upalabyathe

(What can be perceived directly is little and cannot be directly perceived and which is known from scriptures, inference and reasoning)

6. *Ashtangahridaya* 1:2

   Brahma smritva Ayushovedam prajapatim ajigrihatu te ashwino thou sahasraksham te atriputradigan muneem.

   Charaka Su. 1:4.5

   Brahmanahi yadaproktam ayurvedam prajapati Jagraha Nighilena Adhaashwinou thu punasthata ashvibhyam Bhagwan Chakraha pratipedheha kevalam rishiprokto Bharadwaja tasmad sakramupagatam.

   (Brahma expounded the knowledge which was acquired by Daksha prajapati and two Ashwins. From Ashwin twins Shakra (Indra) acquired it and later by Bharadwaja).

7. *Sushruta* Su. 15

   Ihaghalyayurvedo Namopangam Atharva vedasya

   (In this world, the science of Ayurveda is a supplement of Atharvaveda).

8. *Charaka* Su. 30:31

   swalpam asanniktam sarvadu sarvatomughampakshara

   (A *sutra* (stanza) should be brief containing few letters. It should not be doubtful in meaning and should contain the essence of the subject).

9. *Sushruka Su.* 1:6

   Thataha Alpayushtwam alpamedatvam cha alokya narana bhooyaha ashtata praneetavan

   (Having seen the short span of life and limited intelligence of men, (Brahma) composed *Ayurveda*).

10. *Ashtangahridayam* 1:6

    kaya bala graha urdhwange salya drumshta Jaravrushan Ashtanvangani Tasyahu Chikitsa yeshu samshrita.

    Charaka Su 30:28

    Thasya Ayurvedasya Ashtangan ashtou thad yada kayachikitsa, salakya, salyapahruthikam, vishogrg vairodika

prasamanam, bhutavidhya, kowmarabhrutyakam, rasayanani, vajeekaranam idi.

Ayurveda has eight branches as follows- *Kayachikitsa* (General Medicine), *shalakyam* (ENT & Cephalic Diseases), *Shalyapahartrikom* (Surgery), *vishagara vairodika prasamanam* (Toxicology), *bhutavidya* (Psychiatry), *koumarabhrityakom* (Pediatrics), *rasayana* (rejuvenation) and *vaijikaranam* (Aphrodisiac).

11. Dahanukar, Sharadini & Thatte, Urmila, (2000); *Ayurveda Revisited*, Popular Prakshan, Bombay, p. 16.
12. Murthy, N.A. & Pandey, D.P., (2000); *Ayurvedic Cure for Common Diseases*, Orient Paper Backs, New Delhi, p. 18.
13. Warrier, Krishnankutty N.V., (1980); *Ayurveda Charitram*, Malayalam, p. 341.
14. *Ibid.*, p. 344.
15. *Ibid.*, p. 339.
16. *Charaka* su. 1: 40

    Sarira Indriya sattwa atma Samyogodari Jeevitam.

    (Life is combination of *Sharira* (the body) *indriya* (the senses), *atma* (the soul) and *manas* (mind).
17. Joshy, V. Sunil, (1998); *Ayurveda and Panchakarma*, Motilal Banarsidas Publishers, New Delhi, p. 16.
18. *Ibid.*, p. 21.
19. *Ibid.*, p. 29.
20. *Sushruta Samhita Sarreram* I chapter III paragraph:

    Thadyada Prithvi-ap-tejo-vayu-Akashani

    (The five elements are earth, water, fire, air, and ether (space)
21. *Susruta* Su: 1:22

    Asmin sasthree panchamahabhuta sareeri samavayu Purushaha.

    (Ayurveda deals with the human being who is made up of soul and *panchamahabhutas*).

22. *Ashtangahridaya* Su.11.1
Doshadhatu mala moolam sada dehasya
(Dosha, dhatu and mala are the fundamental units of the body)

23. *Charaka* Su.9:4
Vikarodhatu Vaishamyam
(The disequilibrium of *dhatu* results in disease)
Charaka Su.9:4
Dhatusamyam prakrutiruchiyathe
(The equlibrium of *dhatu* is said to be normal health)

24. *Ashtangahridaya* Su.1:13
Rasasrukmamsa mede asthi majja sukrani dhathava
(*Rasa, rakta, mamsa, meda, asthi, majja* and *shukra* are the seven *dhatus*).

25. *Ashtangahridaya* Su. 11:13
(Urine, faecal matter and sweat are the malas)

26. *Ashtangahridaya* Su.1:7
Vada pitta kapham che idi triodoshasamsada
(*Vata, pitta* and *kapha* are the three doshas).

27. *Ashtangahridaya* Su. 1:20
sthudosha Vaishamyam
Doshasamyam Arogadha
(Disease is the disequilibrium of doshas. The balanced state of doshas is health).

28. *Ashtangahridaya* Su.1:10
Suklaartha vastair Janmadhou Visheneva Vishakrime
thaishcha tisra prakrutayo heena madhyothama prithak
samadhatu samasthasu sreshta nindhya dwidoshaja
(The toxins in the sexual secretions of parents results in offsprings with bad characteristics. Similarly the secretions give shape to people with *vatala constitition, pittaprakiti and kapha prakriti*. Presence of all *doshas* is balanced state, while vitiation of two *doshas* is bad)

29. *Sushruta* Su.15:45

Samadosha samagnishcha samadhatu malakriya

prassannatma indriya swastha ithyabhithiyathe)

(The person who has *doshas, agni* (digestive fire), *dhatus and malakriya* and who has sound soul, senses and mind is declared to be healthy)

30. Joshy, V. Sunil, (1998); *Ayurveda and Panchakarma,* Motilal Banarsidas Publishers, New Delhi, p. 89.

31. *Sushruta* Su.4

Thwesham sansodhana samsamana ahara acharaha

(The four methods used for treatment of diseases are *sodhana, shamana, ahara and Vihara.*)

32. *Ashtangahridaya* Su.1

Shodhanam Shamanam Chethi Samasadoushadam dwitha

(The two types of treatments used are *Shodhana* and *Shamanatherapy*).

33. *Ashtangahridaya* Su.3: 30

Sneha Klinna Koshtaga dhatuga va

Sroto leena ye cha shakasthi samtha

Dosha swedai te draveekruthya koshtam.

Neetha samyak shudhibhi Nirhriyanthe

(*Swedana* and *snehana* are *purvakarmas*. It helps to bring the accumulated toxins from the body to the gut)

34. *Ashtangahridaya* su: 38:45

samsodhana sra visrava snehayojana langhanai

yathyagni manthatam tasmad kramam peyadi macharethu

(After doing *shodhana* therapy, the digestive fire will diminish. To overcome this, *paschatkarma* is applied)

35. *Manakkodam Kesvan Vaidyar, Panchakarma Chikitsa*

Vamanam Rechanam Nasya Niruhaschanuvasana

(The panchakarmas are *vamana, virechana, Nasya, Niruha* and *Annuvasana*).

3

Ayurveda as a Catalyst for Tourism Development in Kerala

3.1. Travel History of Kerala

Kerala is known as the land of spices. The need for spices brought people of various nationalities to Kerala. The early traders were the Babylonians, Assyrians, Greeks, Romans, Chinese and the Phoenicians[1]. The Arabs and the Jews followed them. The Portuguese arrived in India in 1498. Vasco da Gama arrived at Kappad near Kozhikode and established the Portuguese rule in Kerala. The Dutch, the French and the British followed them. Evidence indicates that Kerala's foreign contacts increased after the discovery of monsoon winds. The traders and sailors understood that if vessels are moved according to the winds a traveller from the Gulf of Aden can reach the western coast of India or Kerala in forty days. The presence of a large coastline and spices attracted foreigners to Kerala even from 3rd millennium B.C.[2] Arab travellers like Sulaiman, Ibn Batuta,

Rashiduddin and European travellers like Marco Polo, Benjamin of Tudela, John of Monte Corvino etc. visited Kerala in the early centuries[3]. The foreign travellers and traders brought their religions too to Kerala. The religions which reached Kerala through the Arabian Sea were Christianity, Judaism and Islam. The peaceful coexistence of these religions gave shape to a pluralistic society in Kerala.

3.2. Kerala—Salient Features

Kerala is an evergreen state situated on the southern tip of India (see map) with only 1.18 percent of the total area of the country. It accounts for 3.34 percent of the total population of the county. The state economy has been growing at a faster pace averaging 7.8 percent since 2000-01. The growth of population is the lowest among all sates of India. 58.8 percent of the state's income comes from the service sector and this can be mainly attributed to its success in the tourism sector. The service sector engages almost 38 percent of the population with an annual increase of 10.2 percent growth in the sector. The per capita income stands at Rs. 29,601 in the year 2005-06. The literacy rates of 94.2 percent for males and 87.4 percent for females are the highest in India. Kerala has the highest sex ratio in the country, which has increased from 1036 females per1000 males in 1991 to 1058 females per 1000 males in 2001. The state has the lowest infant mortality at 12 deaths per 1000 births. Another notable fact is that 97.7 percent of births are with trained assistance[4]. Thus Kerala ranks at the top of all states in human development indicators. The geographical position of Kerala and its connection with major cities of India are shown in figure 3.1.

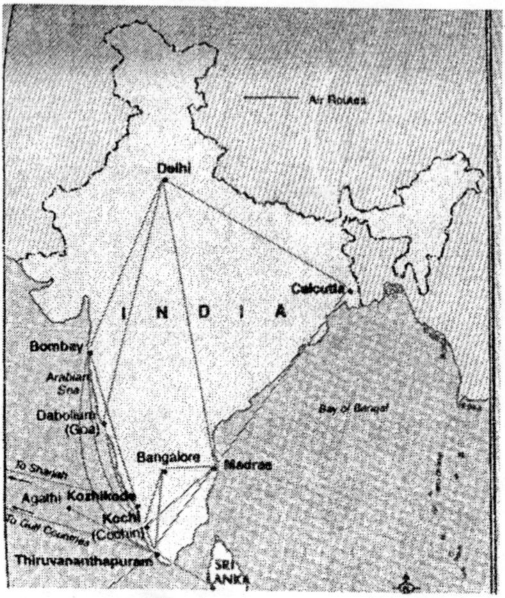

Figure 3.1

Geographical position of Kerala and air routes between important cities of India and Kerala

Source: Tourist Brochure, The Kerala Map, Kerala Tourism.

Kerala (see tourist map) is situated between Arabian Sea on the West and the Western Ghats towering 500 to 2700 meters on the east. It is located in the north latitude between $8^{0}18'$, and $12^{0}48'$ and east longitude between $74^{0}52'$and $77^{0}24'^{5}$. The total area of the state is 38,863 sq. km. The coastline is about 580 km in length while breadth varies from 32 km to 121 km. The state can be divided into four physiographic zones—the Highlands (altitude ranging from 600m to 2500 m), the Midlands (300m to 600m), the Lowlands (30m to 300m) and the coastal plains. For administrative purposes, Kerala is divided into fourteen districts. The details are shown in figure 3.2.

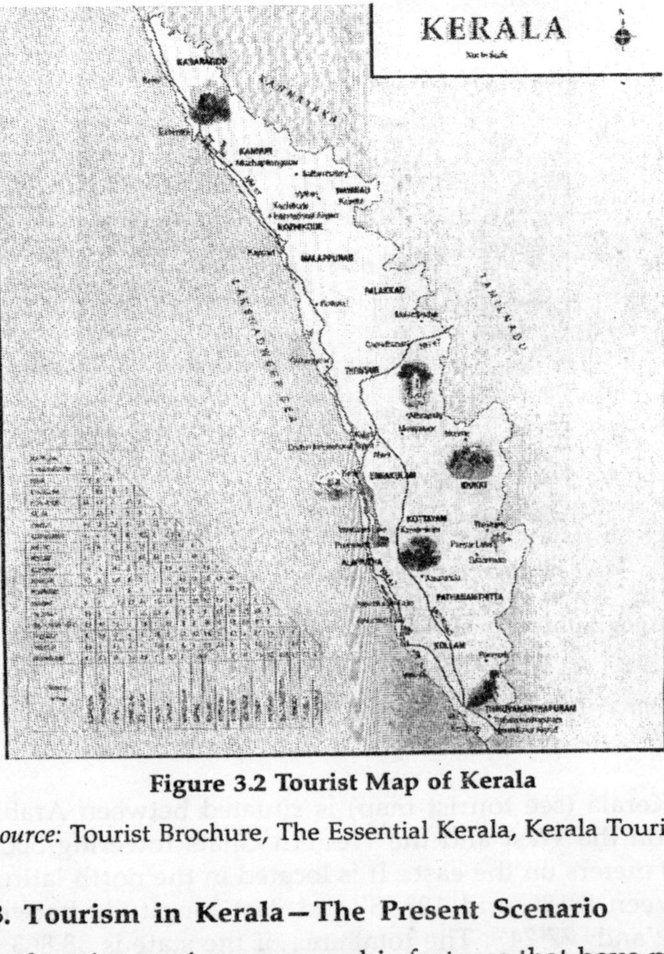

Figure 3.2 Tourist Map of Kerala

Source: Tourist Brochure, The Essential Kerala, Kerala Tourism

3.3. Tourism in Kerala—The Present Scenario

Kerala enjoys unique geographic features that have made it one of the most sought after tourist destinations in the world. Kerala has emerged as the most acclaimed tourist destination of the country in the recent past. World Travel and Tourism Council (WTTC) has selected Kerala as a partner state. National Geographic Traveler, a respected travel magazine after two years of research has chosen Kerala, as one of the fifty must see destinations of life time. They called Kerala as 'One of the ten paradises of the world'. Kerala has also been awarded the 'Best performing

state' award for the year 1999, 2000, 2001 and 2004 by the Government of India[6]. Kerala Tourism has won a number of other awards too from national and international organizations. There are so many countries which develop their tourism industry on the basis of one or two tourist resources which they are having. But, Kerala with a variety of tourist resources can secure a more formidable position in the world tourism map.

With tourism notified as an industry in 1986, the state has focused on connectivity with the world and has three international airports. The airport at Kochi was India's first private airport. Kerala has a large sea port at Kochi and 20 intermediate and small ports. It is a land with long shoreline and serene beaches. Tranquil stretches of backwaters, lush hill stations, exotic wildlife and dense tropical forests, magical festivals, historical and cultural monuments, mist-shrouded mountains, Ayurvedic spas, folklore, music, dance, crafts, spectacular boat races, waterfalls etc. are Kerala's wide range of specialties. In addition to conventionally famous destinations like Kovalam, Varkala and Munnar, tourists show interest in places like Alappuzha, Bekal, Nattika, Thenmala and Wagamon. Eco-tourism along with pilgrim, backwater and village tourism are propelling tourism industry into new levels of progression. Other priority areas are Medical Tourism, Monsoon Tourism and Adventure Tourism. The proposed waterways from Manjeswaram in North Kerala to Kovalam in South Kerala will boost tourism activities in the state.

Tourism in Kerala has recorded remarkable growth in the last so many years. The number of foreign tourists and domestic tourists visiting the state has crossed 4.28 lakhs and 62.71 lakhs respectively. The share of Kerala in foreign tourist arrivals to India is more than 10%[6]. The number of foreign tourists has gone up from a mere 50841 in 1986 to 428534 in the year 2006. Table 3.1 shows a summary of the foreign tourist arrivals to India and Kerala from 1995 to 2006.

Table 3.1
Foreign Tourist Arrivals in India and Kerala (1995-2006)

Year	*Number of Foreign tourists India*	*Kerala*	*Share of Kerala in Indian Tourist market in%*
1995	2123683	142972	6.73
1996	2287860	176855	7.73
1997	2374094	182427	7.68
1998	2358629	189941	8.05
1999	2481928	202173	8.15
2000	2624259	209933	7.99
2001	2537282	208830	8.23
2002	2384364	232564	9.75
2003	2726214	294621	10.81
2004	3367980	345546	10.26
2005	———	346499	———
2006	———	428534	———

Source: Tourist Statistics 1995-2006, Dept. of Tourism, Kerala.

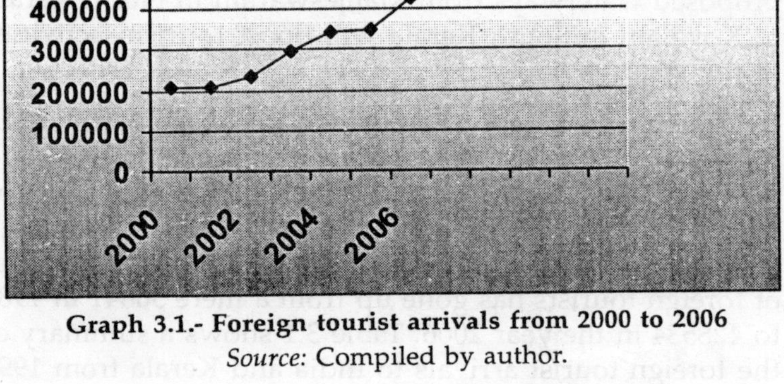

Graph 3.1.- Foreign tourist arrivals from 2000 to 2006
Source: Compiled by author.

Arrivals of domestic tourists to Kerala also showed an upward movement. When the number of domestic tourists who came to Kerala in 1986 was 423756 it became 62,71,724 lakhs in the year 2006. This shows a considerable surge in the number of domestic tourists coming to Kerala. Table 3.2 shows a summary of the domestic tourist arrivals to Kerala during 1995 to 2006.

Table 3.2

Domestic Tourist Arrivals in Kerala from 1995-2006

Year	*Number of Tourists*	*% Variation over the previous year*
1995	3915656	———
1996	4403002	12.45
1997	4953401	12.50
1998	4481714	-9.52
1999	4888287	9.07
2000	5013221	2.56
2001	5239692	4.52
2002	5568256	6.27
2003	5871228	5.44
2004	5972182	1.72
2005	5946623	—
2006	6271724	5.47

Source: Tourist Statistics 1995-06 and Draft Tourism Vision 2025 by Dept. of Tourism, Kerala.

A graphical representation of the pattern of domestic tourist arrivals to Kerala from the year 2000 to 2006 is shown in graph 3.2.

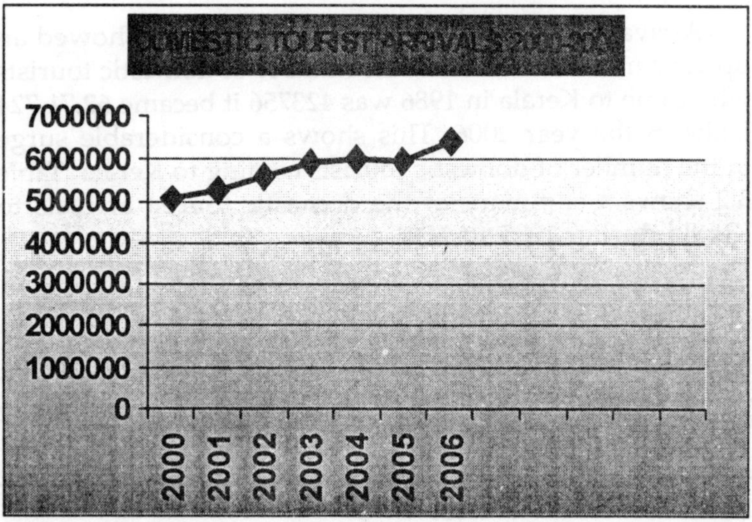

Graph 3.2.

Source: Compiled by author.

A comparative study of foreign tourist arrivals revealed that the following ten countries constituted the maximum share of foreign tourist arrivals to Kerala from 1986 to 1994. The countries are U.K., Germany, France, Italy, U.S.A., Australia, Switzerland, Canada, Japan and Spain. The study also revealed that United Kingdom stands first in the number of its tourists who visited Kerala followed by Germany. The major tourist arrivals to Kerala are from West Europe, North America and Australia. It is illustrated below in figure 3.3.

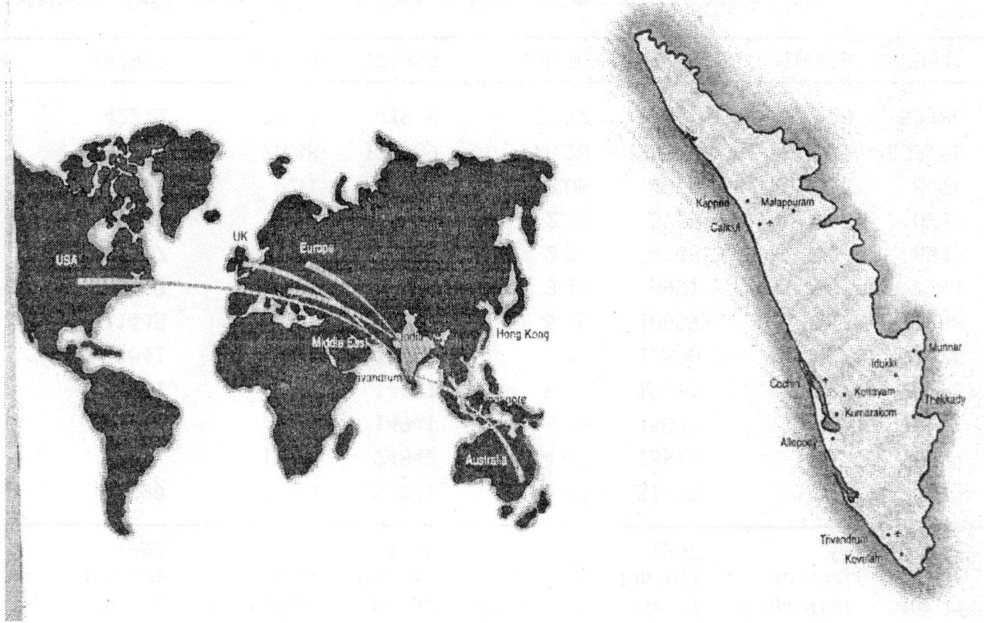

Figure 3.3. Countries generating tourist arrivals to Kerala.
Source: Monsoon Rejuvenation Holidays, Brochure of Department of Tourism, Kerala.

Table 3.3
Summary of the Market Performance of Top Ten Countries, Which Generated Maximum Tourist Arrivals in Kerala from 1995 to 1998

Country	*No. of tourists 1995*	*Proportion to total*	*No. of tourists 1996*	*Proportion to total*	*No. of tourists 1997*	*Proportion to total*	*No. of tourists 1998*	*Proportion to total*
U.K.	28599	20.00	38731	21.90	31472	17.25	34510	18.17
Maldives	14971	10.47	24842	14.05	18818	10.32	18963	9.98
U.S.A.	9363	6.55	14941	8.45	15043	8.25	15301	8.06
Germany	15531	10.86	14421	8.15	15001	8.22	17598	9.26
Sri Lanka	2041	1.43	13800	7.08	12806	7.02	12276	6.46
France	11445	8.01	9863	5.58	10659	5.84	11768	6.20
Italy	5952	4.16	6052	3.42	6971	3.82	7741	4.08
Switzerland	4427	3.10	4770	2.70	4748	2.06	6345	3.34
Japan	5135	3.59	3869	2.19	5755	3.17	6757	3.56
Australia	3296	2.31	3620	2.05	4059	2.22	6494	3.42
Total	100760	70.48	134909	76.28	125362	68.72	133755	72.53
Others	42212	29.52	41946	23.72	57065	31.28	52186	27.47
Grand total	142972	100.00	176855	100.00	182427	100.00	189941	100.00

Source: Tourist statistics 1995, 1996, 1997 and 1998 by Department of Tourism Kerala.

A comparative study of the foreign tourist arrivals to Kerala revealed that countries like U.K, Maldives, U.S.A, Germany, Sri Lanka, France, Italy, Switzerland, Japan and Australia generated the maximum share of tourists from 1995 to 1998. Nationals of U.K. stand first in visiting Kerala followed by nationals of Maldives, U.S.A. and Germany. The study revealed that Western Europe accounted for bulk of the tourists, which amounted to 46.13% in 1995 (65954 tourists), 41.75% in 1996 (73837 tourist), 37.74% in 1997 (68851 tourists) and 41.04% in 1998 (77962 tourists). A summary of the market performance of top ten countries, which generated maximum tourist arrivals to Kerala from 1995 to 1998 are shown in Table 3.3.

A comparative study of the foreign tourist arrivals to Kerala revealed that countries like U.K., France, U.S.A., Maldives, Germany, Italy, Australia, Switzerland, Netherlands and Japan constituted majority of the foreign tourist arrivals to Kerala. The study revealed that tourist arrival from the first ten countries constituted 64% and 66.47% of the total foreign tourist arrivals to Kerala for 2003 and 2004 respectively. United Kingdom remained on the top of all tourist-generating countries for Kerala followed by France, U.S.A., Maldives, Germany etc. The details are shown in Table 3.4.

Table 3.4
Summary of the Market Performance of Top Ten Countries, Which Generated Maximum Tourist Arrivals in Kerala during 2003-2004

Country	*No. of tourists 2003*	*Proportion to total (%)*	*No. of tourists 2004*	*Proportion to total*
U.K.	50363	17.09	61684	17.85
France	30225	10.26	37739	10.92
U.S.A.	25933	8.80	29188	8.45
Maldives	16333	5.54	25863	7.48
Germany	21347	7.25	25304	7.32

Italy	10291	3.49	12688	3.67
Australia	7017	2.38	10271	2.97
Switzerland	10260	3.48	9715	2.81
Netherlands	9379	3.18	9665	2.80
Japan	7463	2.53	7598	2.20
Total	188611	64	229715	66.47
Others	106010	36	115831	33.53
Grand total	294621	100.00	345546	100.00

Source: Tourist Statistics 2004, Department of Tourism, Kerala.

The arrival of foreign tourists to Kerala is in a typical pattern. Despite a slight increase in the arrival of foreign tourists in the beginning of the year, the figure gradually decreases till June, and then a general upward trend is seen except certain months from July onwards. The months of December and January marked the highest international tourist inflow to Kerala. (Table 3.5)

The study of monthwise arrival of domestic tourists to Kerala showed that maximum number of arrivals were in the months of November, December and January. (Table 3.6). Majority of the domestic arrivals are to Guruvayoor followed by Thiruvananthapuram and Kochi. Study of district wise arrival of foreign tourists (2006) to Kerala showed that Thiruvananthapuram received major portion of tourist arrivals. Other leading districts are Ernakulam, Idukki, Alappuzha and Kottayam. Tourist arrivals to these five districts constitute 92.74% of the total arrivals to Kerala. Thrissur district followed by Ernakulam and Thiruvananthapuram received the maximum number of domestic tourists. The average duration of stay of domestic tourists is 6.5 days while that of foreign tourists is 14.1 days.

Table 3.5
Monthwise Arrival of Foreign Tourists in Kerala from 2000 to 2006

Month	*2000*	*2001*	*2002*	*2003*	*2004*	*2005*	*2006*
January	24388	31625	29440	41845	45630	43345	58858
February	23268	30862	29105	36163	43418	41314	56530
March	17499	21957	19246	25261	35006	33479	39584
April	13964	17868	18028	20106	23546	20191	32377
May	12923	10653	10794	12675	14870	14919	20470
June	8306	6571	6610	10820	12734	13239	16209
July	8514	7747	8581	14824	17228	17593	23578
August	17764	13611	14226	19240	27341	24398	28821
September	18222	12391	17808	20253	21103	20064	21888
October	17344	11913	20744	24702	22160	28068	28681
November	22592	19310	26190	32165	38118	42324	44421
December	25149	24322	31792	36567	44392	47565	57117
Total	209933	208830	232564	294621	345546	346499	428534

Source: Tourist statistics 2000-2006 by Department of Tourism, Kerala.

Table 3.6

Monthwise Arrival of Domestic Tourists in Kerala from 1998 to 2004

Months	*1998*	*1999*	*2000*	*2001*	*2002*	*2003*	*2004*
Jan.	354406	453729	454330	472377	471608	511396	523145
Feb.	312576	402718	382657	399215	387550	427116	451420
March	308514	419911	369231	396320	382452	400503	422727
April	330395	456629	453194	498856	499217	514213	503583
May	347725	441644	486006	479515	537429	566603	561503
June	296525	351733	356260	383196	406500	450537	440469
July	287957	356893	361034	396805	406622	421346	508893
August	367812	367486	373599	428291	488050	629920	589182
Septe.	441951	382841	386123	432608	466928	696977	457398
October	421477	403944	433426	427181	472056	513082	516386
Nov.	429204	411233	376877	442386	494481	526578	544746
Dec.	583172	439526	478484	482942	555363	572957	552730
Total	4481714	4888287	5013221	5239692	5568256	5871228	5972182

Source: Tourist Statistics, 1998, 2000 & 2004 by Department of Tourism, Kerala.

Foreign and domestic tourist arrivals to the state show a striking contrast in the preferences of both. The foreigners consider Kochi as the most sought after destination followed by Thiruvananthapuram and Kovalam.

Average duration of stay of foreign tourists in Kerala is 14.1 days. The preferred destinations are Thiruvananthapuram, Kovalam, Kochi, Kumarakom, Alappuzha and Thekkady. The details are shown in the table 3.7.

Table 3.7

Average Duration of Stay at Major Tourist Destinations (Foreign Tourists)

Place	*Average Duration of Stay*
Thiruvananthapuram	4.4
Kovalam	4.6
Kochi	3.5
Kumarakom/Alappuzha	2.4
Thekkady	2.7
Total Kerala	14.1days

Source: Tourist Statistics 1999 & 2000 by Department of Tourism, Kerala.

A comparative study of average duration of stay of domestic tourists in Kerala revealed that the total average duration of stay is 6.5 days. The preferred destinations are Thiruvananthapuram, Kochi, Thekkady, Munnar, Kumarakom, Alappuzha and Guruvayoor. The details are shown in Table 3.8.

Table 3.8

Average Duration of Stay at Major Tourist Destinations (Domestic Tourists)

Place	*Average duration of stay*
Thiruvananthapuram	2.5
Kochi	2.5
Thekkady/Munnar	2.7
Kumarakom/Alappuzha	2.2
Guruvayoor	2.1
Total Kerala	6.5 days

Source: Tourist Statistics 1999 & 2000 by Department of Tourism, Kerala.

A comparative study of the spending pattern and per day expenditure of foreign and domestic tourists revealed the amounts they spent for various items. The foreign tourists are spending a significant amount on hotels, followed by shopping for handicrafts, shopping for other items, local transport and rejuvenation. Per day expenditure of domestic tourists is as low as Rs. 682/- while that of foreign tourists are Rs. 1764.

Foreign tourists coming to Kerala are keen on using different types of accommodations. Majority are interested in staying in conventional hotels while a considerable number of tourists are turning towards innovative tourism experiences by staying in Ayurvedic centers, home stays, tree houses etc.

Table 3.9.

Classification of Foreign Tourists According to the Accommodation Used (2004)

Sl. No.	*Type of accommodation used*	*% of Tourists to total*
1	Heritage	6.78
2	Ayurveda centre	10.86
3	Home Stay	1.09
4	Hotels & Others	81.27
	Total	100.00

Source: Tourist Statistics (2004), Department of Tourism, Kerala.

The amount of earnings from tourism, revenue generated from tourism and the average annual investment for tourism during the year 2006 are shown in table 3.10.

Table 3.10

Tourist Spending and Earnings in 2006

1	Income generated (Foreign Exchange)	Rs. 1988.40crores.
2	Revenue generated from tourism	Rs. 9126 crores.
3	Average annual investment	Rs. 1000 crores.

Source: www.keralatourism.org, Department of Tourism, Kerala.

The study of foreign exchange earnings from 1995 to 2006 from tourism revealed a quantum jump in the earnings which is shown in Table 3.11. In the year 1995, foreign exchange earnings were a meager Rs. 158.76 crores while it reached a mammoth figure of Rs. 1988.40 crores in 2006.

Table 3.11

Foreign Exchange Earnings from Tourism

Year	*Earnings (Rs. in crores)*
1995	158.76
1996	196.38
1997	273.2
1998	302.08
1999	416.07
2000	525.3
2001	535.0
2002	705.67
2003	983.37
2004	1266.77
2005	1552.31
2006	1988.40

Source: Tourist the Statistics 1999 and 2006, Department of Tourism, Kerala.

The state plan allocation for tourism has made a quantum jump in the last nine years from 1996-97 to 2004-05. The plan allocation which was Rs. 29.2 crores in the year 1996-97 increased to Rs. 79.60 crores in the year 2004-05.This had a significant impact on tourism development too. The details are shown in table 3.12.

Table 3.12

Plan Allocation for Tourism from 1996-97 to 2004-05

Year	*Plan allocation (in crores)*
1996-97	29.2
1997-98	36
1998-99	37.2
1999-00	36
2000-01	46
2001-02	40
2002-03	80
2003-04	74.52
2004-05	79.60

Source: Tourist Statistics (2004), Department of Tourism, Kerala.

3.4. Health Holidays

A notable trend in global tourism has been the popularity of health care centers. The tourism trade too has been responsive and is making effort to cater to this ever-growing market. Promotion of physical well being and massage has always been a part of the Asian way of life. The numbers of health and fitness enthusiasts who are using various types of health holidays are increasing all over the world.

Health holiday market is a fairly developed one in various parts of the world. In France the Accor group is devoting full 20 percent of its total investments in the hospitality sector to the development of the health resorts. It is the leader in France in *thalassotherapy* or seawater therapy. The business potential of health holidays is indicated by an Accor survey which shows that at least

20 percent of Europeans are looking for more active, health oriented holidays and would like to find some kind of health and fitness facilities integrated in their holiday resorts or even take their holidays in a dedicated health resort[7].

3.5. Ayurveda and Tourism

Kerala has sensed the potential for health holidays based on its century's old medicinal system, Ayurveda. Holidaying for fitness has struck its roots in Kerala. A number of hotels and resorts along with hospitals are offering this treatment. The market for these types of packages is mainly from Europe and North America[8].

In Kovalam, the ITDC has for some years offered Ayurvedic facilities. Now other agencies at various parts of Kerala are also making arrangements for their guests to obtain services of trained personnel who are proficient in the application of this therapy. Along with the hotels and resorts with star facilities, dedicated Ayurvedic hospitals like Aryavaidyasala at Kottakal near Kozhikode is also attracting fitness enthusiasts and patients.

Various forms of Ayurvedic treatments are offered to the customers, whose duration will also vary according to the nature of treatment. Kerala's equable climate, natural abundance of forests with a wealth of herbs and medical plants are a key to the success of Ayurvedic treatments of Kerala. The treatment is offered during monsoon when the atmosphere remains dust free and cool, opening the pores of the body to the maximum, making it most receptive to Ayurvedic herbal oils and therapy[9].

3.6 Seasonality and Ayurveda

According to various Ayurvedic texts, treatment should only be carried out during *'Nasheethoshnavastha'* i.e., when the atmosphere is not very cold or hot. These texts prescribe the monsoon period as the most suitable time for treatment.

Ayurvedic treatment is popular in Kerala, since the state is having an equable climate. The climate in Kerala is tropical and the temperature varies from 18^{0}C to 35^{0}C which is most suitable for Ayurvedic treatments. Climatic conditions directly influence curing of diseases. *Sodhana* therapy and treatments for rejuvenation can be ideally performed during three months. The three months are mid October to mid November, mid February to mid March and mid July to mid August. Even though the best seasons are prescribed, it is always good to take the treatment at the initial stage of the ailment.

The tourist season in Kerala is from October to March. But Ayurvedic treatments are mainly offered during monsoon months of June, July and August. With the introduction of Ayurveda as a tourism product, tourism activity has become a round the year activity. Ayurvedic therapies emerged big in the tourism sector mainly after Kerala started promoting it. The Ayurvedic centers of Kerala including resorts and hospitals offer Ayurveda treatments with duration of up to fifty-one days.

3.7. Classification Scheme for Ayurveda Centres

The elevation of Ayurveda as a unique selling preposition (USP) of Kerala tourism has brought a substantial increase in the number of Ayurvedic centers in and around all the major tourist destinations in the state. Most of these operate according to their terms and often flout safety and health regulations. To avoid any such misuse and maintain a uniformity of practice, Government of Kerala has brought out a scheme for Approval of Ayurveda centers vide G.O (M.S)140/98/GAD dated 23-03-1998. According to this order, a uniform approval was given to all the centers fulfilling the conditions prescribed, irrespective of its differences in class and quality. Later, the Kerala government came up with a government order G.O (M.S.) 35/2002/GAD dated 28-1-2002, for classifying the Ayurvedic centers into two types named Olive Leaf and

Green Leaf to differentiate them in the level of quality of facilities and services provided. The criteria for Olive Leaf Certificate and Green Leaf certificate are as follows.

3.7.1. Criteria for Olive Leaf Certificate

For obtaining Olive Leaf Certificate for the Ayurveda centers the following criteria are to be fulfilled.

i). Facilities

- Minimum two number of treatment rooms (one for males and one for females) having minimum size of 100 sq. ft with width not less than 8 feet. The rooms should have sufficient ventilation and it should be with attached bathroom of size not less than 20 sq. ft. The toilets should have proper sanitary fittings and floors and walls should be finished with proper tiles.
- One consultation room having minimum size of 100 sq. ft with width not less than 8 feet. The room should be equipped with equipments such as BP apparatus, stethoscope, examination couch, weighing machine etc.
- There should be a separate room of minimum size 100 sq. ft. with width not less than 8 feet, if the centre is not attached with a hotel/resort/hospital.
- There should be separate space/room for preparation of medicine.
- The general construction of the building should be good and locality and environs including immediate approach should be suitable. The furnishing of all the rooms should be good quality. The entire building including the premises should be clean and hygienic.

ii). Equipments

The Centre should have at the following equipments

- One massage table of minimum size 7 feet x 3 feet in each treatment room, made up of good quality wood/fibre glass.
- Gas or electric stove.
- Medicated hot water facility for bathing and other purposes.
- Facilities for sterilization.

iii). Technical Personnel

- There should be at least one full time consultant physician with a recognized degree in Ayurveda.
- The treatments/therapies should be done only under the supervision of a qualified physician with a recognized degree in Ayurveda.
- There should be at least two number of masseurs (one male and one female) having sufficient training from recognized Ayurveda institution by the Government.

iv). Quality of Medicine and Health Programme

- The medicine used should be from an approved and reputed firm. These medicines should be exhibited at the centre.
- The health programmes offered at the centre should be clearly exhibited. The centre should also exhibit the time taken for normal massage and other treatments. The generally approved time limit for a massage is 45 minutes.

3.7.2. *Criteria for Green Leaf certificate*

For Green Leaf Certificate the Ayurveda centre should have the following facilities in addition to all the criteria stipulated for Olive Leaf Certificate.

- The general construction, architectural features etc of the building should be of very high standard. The furnishing, curtains, fittings etc should be with superior quality materials.
- There should be adequate parking space in the premises.
- The bathroom should have bathtubs, and there should be facilities for steam bath.

The following are the additional desirable conditions to get a Green Leaf certificate.

- The centers should be at picturesque locations with greenery in abundance and quiet atmosphere.
- There should be separate hall for meditation/ yoga.
- There should be a herbal garden attached to the center.

3.7.3. *Procedure for classification*

- Every person operating an Ayurveda centre in the State and is desirous to get classification from Department of Tourism, Government of Kerala should apply for classification in the prescribed form.The application form will be available at Directorate of Tourism free of cost. All the application duly filled shall be addressed to Director, Department of Tourism, Park View, Thiruvananthapuram-33.
- A fee of Rs. 2,500/- shall be enclosed with the application form by way of Demand Draft drawn in favour of Director, Department of Tourism, Park View payable at Thiruvananthapuram.

- Director, Tourism shall unless the approval is refused, issue a classification certificate to the centre on the recommendation of a committee consisting of the following members, after inspection.
  - Director, Tourism - Convenor
  - Director, Indian Systems of Medicine - Member
  - Professor Kayachikitsa, Government Ayurveda College, Thiruvananthapuram - Member
  - Representative of Ayurveda College, Kottakkal
  - Representative of Indian Association of Tour Operators (IATO) - Member
- The period of classification will be only for three years. After the expiry of the classification period the centre has to apply for re-classification afresh. In case of Ayurveda centers already approved by Department of Tourism under the existing scheme have to apply for classification afresh if they desire to get classified. Otherwise these approved units will be separately considered as only 'approved Ayurveda centers' till the expiry of the period of approval.
- The Department has prescribed regulatory conditions to be abided by promoters of classified Ayurveda centers. The promoters should furnish the acceptance of these regulatory conditions in the prescribed form.

3.7.4. *Incentives to classified Ayurveda Centers*

Only the Ayurveda centers, which are classified/ approved by Department of Tourism, will be eligible for claming 10% state investment subsidy or electric tariff concession offered by department of tourism, Government of Kerala. Only these centers will be considered for giving publicity and promotion through print and electronic media by the department. Government of Kerala came up with G.O. (M.S.) 331/98/GAD dated 28-04-98 granting

investment subsidy and other concessions to Ayurvedic centers at par with hotels.

3.7.5. Regulatory Conditions for Classification of Ayurveda Centres

All the Classified Ayurveda Centers by Department of Tourism are required to furnish the following information.

- Document relating to legal status i.e. if the company incorporated under the companies Act, a copy of the Memorandum & Articles of Association; if it is a partnership firm, a copy of the partnership deed and the certificate of Registration under the Partnership Act ; if it is a proprietary concern, name and address of the proprietor etc.
- The Centre will submit the following information to the Director, Department of Tourism so as to reach him on or before 31st May every year for the proceedings financial year.

A Bank certificate in regard to foreign exchange deposited by the centre, if any

- ➢ The statement on the number of foreign and domestic tourists treated/handled by the centre during the year.
- ➢ A specimen copy of the health programme with their current tariff card.
- ➢ List of name of the following personnel with their designation, experience etc.
  - Doctors
  - Nurses
  - Masseurs
  - Other, if any
- ➢ Annual report of the centre and a statement showing the balance sheet and profit and loss account within 4 months of the financial year.

- Following the Kerala tradition, male patients will

be massaged by male and female patients by female masseurs. Only trained masseurs will be engaged for the purpose by the centre.

- The Director, Department of Tourism, Government of Kerala should be kept informed from time to time about facilities introduced or withdrawn and of any addition or alteration in regard to the capacity of the centre.
- The tariff should be prominently displayed. The tariff card shall also indicate sales tax, service charges etc.
- Any license and or certificate required from the local administration/police and or other concerned authorizes for the construction/operation of the centre should be obtained directly by the promoters from the concerned authorities. The classification by this Department will not in any way substitute for them. The Department classification will be deemed to have been withdrawn in case of violation of this condition when brought to notice.
- The centre should at all times adhere to the high standards of maintenance and service for which it has been recognized and in all dealings with its guests observe business practices worthy of an establishment of repute.
- Officers of Department of Tourism or any other officer deputed by the Department to inspect the centre premises from time to time will be allowed free access with or without prior notice.

As a result of the introduction of various government rules mentioned above, a group of approved ayurvedic centers came up in Kerala. They are offering a variety of treatments according to the rules and regulations, mentioned in the various government orders.

Out of the 70 approved Ayurvedic centers of Kerala,

41 got Green Leaf certificate while 29 got Olive Leaf certificate. Most of the centers are situated in are situated in Ernakulam, Thiruvananthapuram, Kollam, Kottayam and Alappuzha districts.

Ayurvedic health holidays can attract huge inflow of tourist arrivals to Kerala. A variety of Ayurvedic treatments are offered in Kerala only. The stalwarts of Ayurveda in Kerala have given shape to certain unique treatment methods. Development of Ayurveda as a tourism product will immensely help the state economy through foreign exchange earnings. It can offer employment to a number of people. The increasing number of fitness and health holiday enthusiasts to Kerala shows the potential of Ayurvedic holidays of Kerala. The new tourists who seeks adventure and the unknown including different culture, cuisine, lifestyle, health systems etc has popularized the Ayurvedic health holidays of Kerala all over the world.

References

1. Menon, Sreedhara, A. (1996); *A Survey of Kerala History*, S. Viswanathan Pvt. Ltd., Madras, p. 59.
2. *Ibid.*, p. 59.
3. *Ibid.*, pp. 28-30.
4. *Kerala-Performance, Facts and Figures* (2007), Pearson Education, Delhi.
5. Menon, Sreedhara, A. (1996); *A Survey of Kerala History*, S. Viswanathan Pvt, Ltd. Madras, p. 1.
6. *Tourist Statistics* (2004); Department of Tourism, Kerala.
7. *Kerala Draft Tourism Vision 2025* (2001); Department of Tourism, Kerala, p. 23.
8. *Promote Health Holidays* (1998); Express Travel and Tourism, Bombay, February 16.
9. *Promote Health Holidays* (1998); Express Travel and Tourism, Bombay, February 16.
10. *Monsoon Rejuvenation Holidays*; Brochure of Department of Tourism, Kerala, p. 3.

4

Ayurvedic Tourism: Resources and Facilities in Kerala

4.1. Introduction

The contribution of Kerala in the field of Ayurveda is unique. Ayurveda developed in Kerala with more dedication than other parts of the country. Kerala's Ayurvedic system is not fundamentally different from the main stream. Along with *Charaka Samhitha* and *Sushruta Samhita, Ashtanga Hridaya* and *Ashtanga Sangraha* written by Vagbhata are used by the proponents of Ayurveda in Kerala. But a number of treatment methods which cannot be seen in the Samhitas were developed and followed in Kerala.

The various types of Ayurvedic treatments designed in Kerala have enriched Ayurveda as a system of medicine. A lot of Ayurvedic research took place in Kerala, especially during the ancient period. While in most parts of India where individuals conducted research, in Kerala an eminent group of personalities known as *"Ashtavaidyas"* came

together to conduct group research and development[1]. They were called "*Ashtavaidyas*" since they were the persons who mastered the eight braches of Ayurveda and as they treated according to *Ashtangahridaya*[2]. Patronising of Ayurveda by the *Ashtavaidyas* led to quick growth of the ayurvedic system of medicine in Kerala and even resulted in a special method of treatment known as *Malabar special treatment*[3].

4.2 Ayurveda and Rejuvenation

Ayurveda is nature's gift for rejuvenation and revitalization. Longevity is the ultimate goal of all medical systems. Diseases are hurdles in the path of longevity. It makes both the psyche and the physique uneasy. Uneasy mind and body, adversely affect health and longevity. Ayurveda, a holistic system offers various types of Ayurvedic products to ensure longevity and rejuvenation.

4.3 Rasayanachikitsa

Rasayana is the method of treatment which strengthens all the tissues of the body. It offers a way for rejuvenating the body and restores spirit and vitality resulting in longevity. An elaborate description of this process of revitalization has been given in the classical texts. According to Charaka, this miraculous change can be brought about if "a man with resolution and purpose, full of faith and with no sins of the heart and he who wishes for the wellbeing of all creatures" undergoes a prescribed six month course of rejuvenation.

Types of Rasayanachikitsa

The Rasayanachikitsa for rejuvenation is generally divided into two—*Kudipravesikam* and *Vatatapikam*[4]. Currently Rasayanachikitsa is identified with the first one. These treatments are offered for rejuvenation and also for the cure of diseases. Well equipped *kudi* (building for

rehabilitation), specially made for treatment purpose is required. The recipient of treatment shall remain for the entire duration of the treatment in the specially made room consuming only the prescribed food products which may range from *Chyavanaprash*, milk, *navararice* etc[5]. The duration of *Rasayanachikitsa* is generally one month. The stress and strains of modern life and its harmful after effects in the form of various diseases can be avoided by applying Rasayana Chikitsa. Revival of this disciplined process of classical ayurvedic rejuvenation therapy to the dedicated aspirants will help to solve the pressing health problems of many.

4.4 Panchakarma Treatment in Kerala

The ayurvedic rejuvenative treatment widely practiced today is called *Panchakarma*. This five fold treatment is designed for *shodhana,* the eradication of the cause of the disease. *Panchakarma* has only been intended for the elimination of the disease-causing toxins but also to replenish the body tissues with nourishment. This is why it is often termed as rejuvenation therapy. The proponents of Ayurveda in Kerala developed and offered *Panchakarma* treatment and other allied treatment procedures with at most dedication.

Panchakarma, the foremost purification therapy was introduced by Charaka and Shusruta. Charaka considered *Vamana* (emesis), *Virechana* (purgation), *Niruha Vasti* (non-oily herbal enema), *Annuvasana Vasti* (oily enema) and *Nasya* (Head evacuation) as the five fold *Panchakarma* treatment[6]. Understanding that vitiation of blood could also be a causative factor for certain diseases, Sushruta, father of surgery, devised surgical venesection for letting out vitiated blood. Later the Sushruta School combined the two main divisions of *Vasti* into one category and added *Rakta Mokshana* or letting out the vitiated blood as the fifth division of *Panchakarma.*

4.4.1 *Application of Panchakarma*

Panchakarma therapy is performed in three stages[7]

- *Purvakarma* (pre-operative procedures)
- *Pradhana karma* (operative procedures)
- *Paschat karma* (post-operative procedures)

Purvakarma is the preparatory procedure which prepares the body for the discharge of toxins through *Snehana* (internal and external oleation) and *Swedana* (therapeutic sweating). *Swedana* is the therapeutic application of heat to the body which helps the expulsion of toxins. This process can be further accelerated by *Panchakarma* procedures. A variety of preparatory procedures can be used not only to increase elimination of toxins along with *Panchakarma*, but to rejuvenate specific zones of the body. A variety of procedures which can be used independently and also along with *Panchakarma* is widely used in Kerala.

Purvakarama

Purvakarma procedures are broadly divided into three- *Pachana, Snehana & Swedana.*

I. Pachana (Use of digestives)

In this process, drugs are given to help digestion of ama present in the stomach in the indigested form.

II. Snehana (Oleation)

Oleation is carried out in the patients in two ways.

- *Bahya Snehana*
- *Abhyantara Snehana*

i). Bahya Snehana (External oleation)

In *Bahya Snehana,* oils prepared with herbal decoctions are massaged over the body. These saturate the body and liquefy *ama* present in the *srotas* (body channels).

Types of **Bahyasnehana**

a. Pichu

Pichu is a special treatment for ailments in the head region. This treatment is good for ailments affecting the cranial nerves due to vata disorders. The treatment is named after the folded piece of cloth used to cover the crown called the *Pichu*. The cloth is folded to a thickness equal to that of the palm and of a size that is just enough to cover the head[9].

In this treatment the patient is seated in a chair in an upright position. After preparatory procedures like an oil massage, the prescribed oil is applied on the head. A head band is then tied around the head just above the level of the ears. The *pichu* is then dipped in the medicated oil, spread over the head and oil poured on it till it is totally drenched. After a while, the *pichu* is replaced with a new one, and the process is repeated.

b. Abhyanga

Abhyanga is the process of rubbing medicated oil over the entire body. The oil should be lukewarm with good smell. The anointing must be done especially to ears and foot. Hot oils must not be applied on the head. After a while, the oil is thoroughly washed off using medicated shampoo powder for the body and medicated shampoo for the head. This type of oleation serves as an absolute preventive measure against many ailments related to *vatadosha*. It is also a good preventive against skin diseases and improves skin complexion. Application of oil on the head induces good sleep and also enhances eye sight. It tones up the tissues of the body. It is not suited for those suffering from ailments due to the vitiation of *Kapha dosha*. The application of *abhyanga* is shown in Figure 4.1.

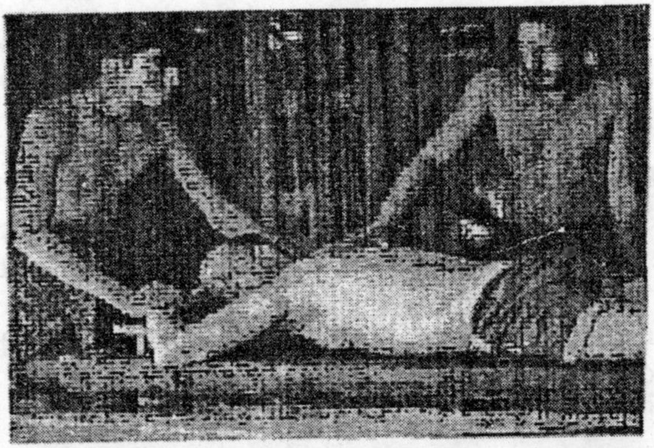

Figure 4.1 Application of abhyanga treatment
Source: Ayurveda, Brochure of Sree Sankara Community for Ayurveda Consciousness Ltd., Changanacherry, Kerala.

ii) Abhyantara Snehana (Internal Oleation)

In this treatment, *Snehas* (lubricants) are administered internally to liquefy the ama in the various *srotas*(body channels) of the system. This is also known as *Snehapanam*. Ghee is considered to be the best of all *Snehas*, as it can retain any properties transmitted to it from other drugs by boiling with it.

iii) Swedana (Sweating or Sudation)

The act of producing sweat on a part or whole of the body is known as *swedanakarma*. The prominent among them are *Navarakizhi, Bashpasweda, Nalisweda, Avagahasweda, Upanahasweda, Patrasweda, Dhara,* and *Pizhichil*. These various treatments followed in Kerala dilate the body's *shrotas* or channels resulting in *ama's* expulsion from the *dhatus*. The heating action of *swedana* results in liquefaction of ama. Dilating the body's internal channels creates a freer pathway for the removal of toxins and waste products. As ama leaves, rigidity and stiffness in the *dhatus* will reduce giving the body greater flexibility. The prominent *swedana* procedures are the following.

a. Navarakizhi (Pindasweda)

Navarakizhi is an important *swedana* which is used not only as a part of *Panchakarma* but also as an effective treatment for many diseases due to *vata* disorders, including hemiplegia, rheumatism, joint pains etc. Here, a bundle of linen filled with a bolus of *navara* or *shastika* rice that has been cooked with milk and herbal decoction is used for fomentaion[10]. This fist sized bundle containing medicine is known as *Kizhi.*

For an effective *Navarakizhi,* five people are required to attend the patient. Two attendants stand on either side of the patient. As a preparatory procedure, medicated oil is applied to his head and body before applying rice bolus to the body. The patient is made to lie on a *droni,* a special wooden bed used for the treatment. When the bolus has warmth that could be comfortably borne by the patient, the body is massaged with it by the attendants. The direction of massage should always be downwards and begins from the neck area. The duty of the fifth person is to facilitate change over of dry linen bags with new ones that have been dipped in warm medicated ointment (*Kuzhambu*) which is kept at a constant temperature. The therapists use their right hands to foment the patient and simultaneously massage with their left hands using similar motions.

To ensure that no area of the body is untouched there are seven standard positions that a patient is made to adopt during treatment. These include sitting, lying on the back, lying on one side, lying on the back again, lying on the other side, lying with face down and finally, lying on the back. Massage is done in all these positions. Massage in each posture is maintained for about 15 minutes. The whole process takes about an hour and three quarters. The course of this treatment may be increased or decreased according to the general condition and health of the patient.

After the fomentation the paste (*kuzhambu*) is removed

slowly. After this, the body and head shall be cleaned and bath should be taken in warm water which is prepared with *'Vatha hara dravyas'* (anti rheumatic drugs). This treatment may be done for a period of seven to twenty one days as is required according to the physical condition of the patient and nature of diseases. The application of a *Navarakizhi* is shown in figure 4.2.

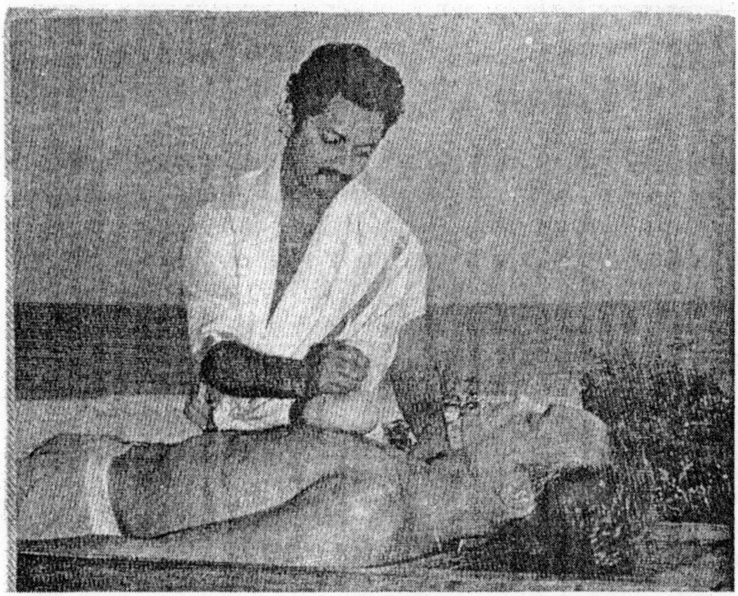

Figure 4.2 Application of Navarakizhi treatment
Source: Ayurvedic Health Holidays in Kerala, Brochure by Department of Tourism, Kerala.

Benefits of Navarakizhi

The effects of treatment if properly done are as follows:

- Removes stiffness to joints due to diseases of vitiated *vata*.

- Cleanses the *srotas* (lymph channels) of the body and brings about good blood circulation.
- It increases appetite.
- It improves complexion
- Improves digestion
- It removes sluggishness of excessive sleep.

Navarakizhi cures all type of diseases of the nervous system including chronic rheumatism, joint pains etc.

b. *Ooshmasweda or Bashpasweda (Steam Bath)*

Bashpa literally means steam. In *Bashpasweda*, the patient is made to either sit in or lie on his back in a specially made box, with only his head outside. Herbal steam is released into the box for a specific time. To avoid dehydration, the patient is given cool liquids before administering *Bashpasweda*. The duration of the treatment is seven to ten minutes or until sweat begins to bead over the patient's body. After the treatment the patient should feel light and enthusiastic as the heat liquefies ama and its heaviness decreases. But this treatment is not advisable for people with heart disease or hypertension.

c. *Nalisweda*

In *Nalisweda*, steam of boiling herbal decoction is applied on the affected area through the nozzle of a tube (*nali*) which penetrates into the tissues along with the oil smeared on the body to produce healing effects[11]. As of now, this process is facilitated by the use of a pressure cooker and nylon reinforced plastic hose which eases the steam's application to the body's surface. Although this type of treatment is given to the whole body, it focuses on the thick and complex structures of the joints to improve their mobility. Generally this treatment lasts for five to seven minutes. It can be used individually out side the *Panchakarma* process. It can be used along with *Snehana* for reducing pain, backaches etc.

d. *Avaghasweda*

The patient is made to sweat while sitting in a tub filled with medical decoction. This kind of *sweda* is good for rheumatism, hernia, painful urination etc.

e. *Upanahasweda*

In *upanahasweda,* a warm mixture of medicated paste and herbal oils is applied on the affected part, covered with cloth or leaves and then tied up. The wrapping is kept on for nearly 12 hours.

f. *Patrasweda or Ilakkizhi*

In this treatment, finely chopped leaves warmed in medicated oil are put on a piece of linen and a fist sized bundle is made. This is used for fomentation. In cases of rheumatism and other diseases due to disorder of the *vata,* fomentation in the affected area brings great relief.

g. *Podikkizhi or Churnasweda*

A linen bag filled with *Churna* (medicated powder) is periodically dipped in herbal decoctions and used for fomentation. The duration of the treatment varies according to disease conditions, up to maximum of one hour. After fomentation, a normal bath is recommended followed by a diet regimen for a few days. *Podikhizhi* is effective for ailments due to *vata* or *kapha* disorders.

4.5 Dhara

Dhara is the process of pouring medicated liquid over the patient's body. This is one of the prominent Ayurvedic treatments offered in Kerala. *Dhara* is divided into three types—*Shirodhara, Sarvangadhara* and *Pizhichil*[12]. They are further divided into three depending on the type of medicine and liquid used. *Snehadhara* which is *dhara* with various medicated oils, *Takradhara,* with butter milk mixed

with a medicated decoction and *Ksheeradhara* with milk mixed with a medicated decoction. This process lasts for one to one and a half hours. The treatment is done for a period of 7 to 14 days either in the morning or in the evening. *Dhara* improves sleep, eye sight, gives cooling effect to head and cures sinusitis and headaches.

i. Shirodhara or Moordhanya Dhara

In *Shirodhara,* the oil is poured on the forehead of the patient. *Shiro* means "head" and *dhara* means "the dripping of oil like a thread". This treatment drips warm oil in a steady stream on the forehead. After the preparatory application of oil on the head, the patient is made to lie on this back on a *droni* (wooden plank) with the vessel for the *dhara,* hung six to eight inches above his forehead. A head band is tied around the forehead just above the eyebrows to prevent oil from flowing into the eyes. The warm oil from the vessel is then let out in a continual flow through a spout at the bottom. *Shirodhara* is usually given for twenty minutes, three to four times during a seven day treatment period.

Shirodhara is very effective for treating diseases affecting the head, eyes and the nervous system. *Shirodhara* is useful for treating sinusitis and certain cases of insanity. The oils used for *dhara* calms and nourishes the nervous system. It also improves memory. The application of a *shirodhara* is shown in figure 4.3.

ii. Sarvangadhara (Snehadhara)

In *Sarvangadhara,* oil is poured over the entire body with simultaneous massaging. Oil should be applied on the head of the patient before starting the *dhara*. The patient is made to lie on a *droni* and two attendants each stand on either side, one to oil the upper portion of the body and the other, the lower. Nozzled mud pitchers (*kindis*) are used for pouring the oil. The oil should be kept warm throughout the course of the treatment. While the

attendants pour oil with their right hands they also massage the patient using their left hands. The fifth attendant replaces empty pitchers with new ones. The flow of oil over the body should continue for a specific period and no area should be left uncovered.

After the *dhara,* the body is wiped with towel. For removing the oil from the body and the hair, green gram paste and some herbal shampoo are usually used. After the bath, usually *Rasnadi churna,* is applied on the forehead to absorb moisture.

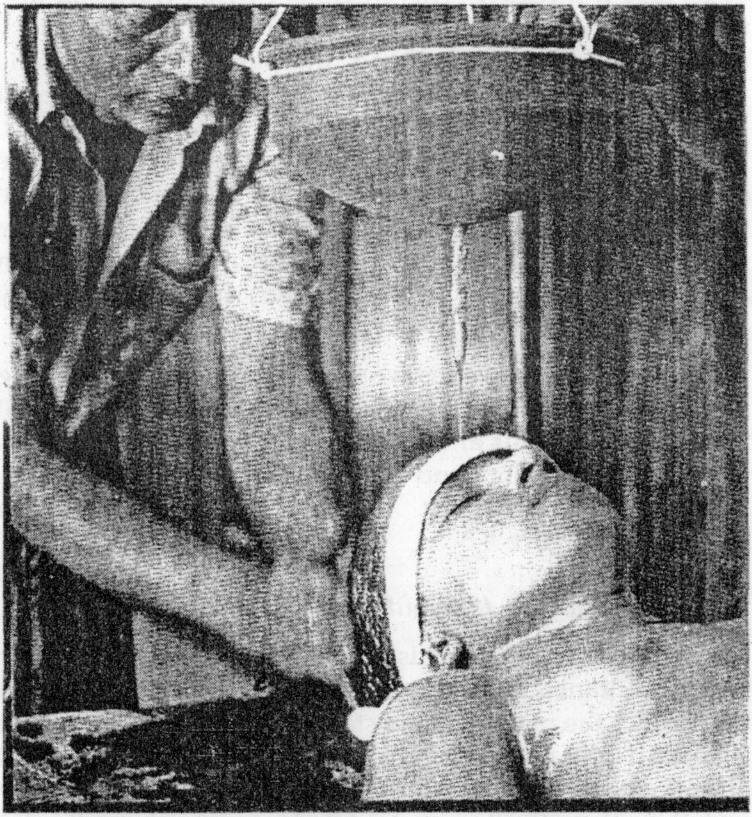

Figure 4.3 The application of shirodhara treatment.
Source: Ayurveda, Brochure of Sree Sankara community for Ayurveda Consciousness Ltd., Changanacherry, Kerala

iii. Pizhichil (Kayaseka)-Oil Bath

Pizhichil is a process of sudation by which the body is made to perspire by means of the application of warm medicated oil. *Pizhichil,* literally means squeezing and is a unique contribution of Kerala. After seating the patient in a wooden basin, a paste prepared with medicated oil and medicated powder is applied on the centre of the head. Then warm medicated oil is squeezed over the patient's body from a piece of cloth that is periodically dipped in the vessel containing the oil[13]. The oil is to be poured at a medium speed and from a moderate height from the body. Depending on the conditions of the patient and ailment, the physician prescribes the most suited medicated oil to be squeezed on the body.

Four attendants under the supervision of a physician perform the treatment. The attendants while applying the oil have at the same time to massage the body of the patient gently with their left hands in downward strokes. This process must be carried out in seven standard positions to ensure that no area of the body is left uncovered. This process is to be done for one to one and a half hours increasing the time gradually daily. This treatment can be held for a period of 7 to 14 days. The patient needs to have rest and absolute peace of mind during the duration of treatment.

Although *Pizhichil* is a process of sudation used as a *Purvakarma* treatment, it has also been proved to be highly effective on its own for treating diseases caused due to vitiation of the *vata* humor, especially hemiplegia, paralysis, rheumatoid arthritis, muscle spasms and other degenerative diseases affecting muscles. The application of *Pizhichil* treatment is shown in figure 4.4.

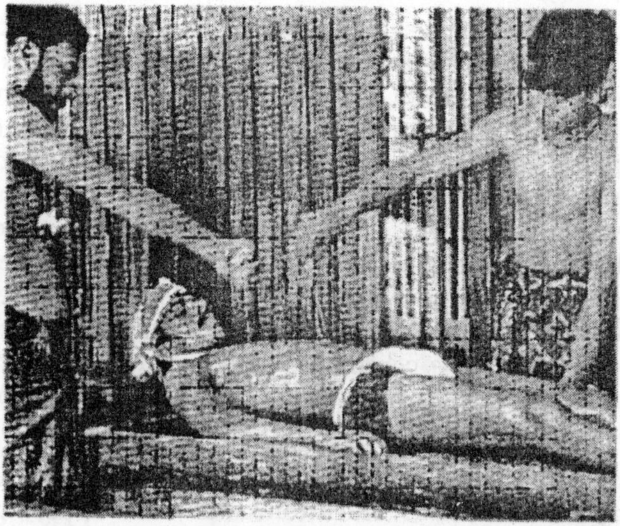

Figure 4.4 The application of Pizhichil treatment.

Source : Ayurveda, Brochure of Sree Sankara community for Ayurveda Consciousness Ltd., Changanacherry, Kerala.

4.6 Panchakarma

The five types of *Panchakarma* are *vamana, virechana, nasya, vasti* and *raktamokshana.*

4.6.1 *Vamana (Therapeutic Emesis)*

Vamana is the pacificator process used for the expulsion of vitiated *kapha*[14]. This is a drug induced emetic process. *Vamana* is done not only in diseased state but also in normal persons for maintaining the health especially in *"vasantha ritu"* (March-May). *Vamana* cures diseases like arthritis, asthma, acne, chronic cold, diabetes and other various *kapha* disorders.

a. Purva Karma (pre-operative procedure)

The patient must be treated by external and internal oleation. For lubricating the body internally, medicated ghee according to the condition of the patient should be given in small doses for seven days. Then the patient is subjected to the next stage of the therapy, sweating which mobilizes the liquefied ama and directs it to the *koshta* (stomach). From there it can be thrown out during the *pradhanakarma*.

b. Paradhana Karma (operative Procedure)

The night before starting the *Pradhanakarma*, the patient is given *kapha* exciting food like yoghurt, bananas, milk, black gram soup etc. In the next morning the patient is given approximately 300 ml. of porridge made from wheat and milk to promote watery secretions. After consuming the porridge the patient is administered the emetic which can be *Madana* (Randia Dumetorum), *Vacha* (Acorus Calamus) or *Aamalaka* (Emlica officinale).

After the administration of *Vamana* drugs the patient shall be observed for around 45 minutes for the onset of certain symptoms like perspiration, nausea etc. which indicates the movement of *doshas* to the *koshta* (stomach). Then the patient starts to vomit. To stimulate further vomiting, the patient is given diluted milk at intervals. Once the vomiting ceases, the physician observes the quantity of vomitus. In a successful emesis, the quantity of vomitus is more. *Kapha* related impurities are eliminated through the *vamana* procedure.

c. Paschat Karma (post-operative procedure)

After emesis, the patient is made to inhale medicated smoke, which is known as *Dhoomapana*. After this the patient is made to take complete rest. Loud talking, too much eating, travelling, sexual intercourse, exposure to sun and dust etc. are to be avoided after *vamana* procedure.

Vamana should not be performed on weak people, children, pregnant women and those suffering from hepatitis and tuberculosis.

4.6.2. *Virechana (Purgation Therapy)*

The process by which the *pitta* related toxins are eliminated from the body is called *Virechana*[15]. This process cleanses small intestine and *pitta* dominant organs like liver and gallbladder, which is situated in the mid-zone of the body. In *Virechana*, drugs that stimulate bowel movements are induced for the expulsion of excess *pitta* and other *doshas* via the rectum.

a. *Purvakarma*

Internal and external oleation (*snehana*) followed by therapeutic sweating (*swedana*) are essential before *Virechana*. If the patient has undergone *vamana*, the next treatment of any kind including *virechana* should be after 15 days. Even if the patient has undergone *snehana* and *swedana* during *vamana*, they must be carried out again before *virechana*. Full oleation is essential to dislodge ama and toxins and draw them into the small intestine, which will be ultimately expelled by *Virechana*. For lubricating the body internally, medicated ghee should be given in small doses for three days according to the condition of the patient. Sudation should be done for the next two days.

b. *Pradhana Karma*

On the day of *Virechana*, suitable dose of purgative is to be given only after confirming proper digestion of last day's meal. In Kerala, the usual practice is to give the purgatives around 6 A.M. in the morning. After two hours, the purgation process will start. In between, lukewarm water should be given to the patient in small quantity. Ideally, the patient experiences 6 to 8 bowel movements. When all the toxins have been expelled from the small intestine, the urge to evacuate will subside. The purgative

sis prepared using roots and fruits of herbs like *Trivrit* (Ipomoea Turpetum), *Jayapala* (Croton Tinglium), *Aragvadha* (Cassia Fistula) etc.

Virechana is effective for treating chronic headaches, jaundice, diabetes, spleen enlargement, arthritis, asthma etc. and all types of intestinal disorders. *Virechana* should not be used on infants, elderly and pregnant women.

4.6.3. *Nasya (Errhine Therapy)*

Nasya is the process by which medical oils or powders are administered through the nostrils. Ayurveda consider nose as the doorway to the brain. *Nasya* cleanses and opens the channels of the head and it is an important treatment method for illness of the head region. If *Nasyakarma* is done properly and regularly, it will keep the person's eyes, nose and ear unimpaired. *Nasya* is good for chronic sinusitis, head ache, migraine, eye diseases, and cervical spondylitis etc[16].

Nasya Karma Procedure

Nasya is carried out in three stages of *Purvakarma, Pradhanakarma* and *Paschatkarma.* Before *nasya,* is administered warm herbalised oil is massaged into the face focusing on the sinus area for sweating. The patient is made to lie down on his back with his head slightly bent back. After this, slightly warm herbalised oil is dripped into both nostrils. To draw the oil more deeply into nasal passageways, the patient inhale and releases it suddenly. He must spit out all the impurities and medicine that reaches his mouth. After the treatment, the neck, cheeks and fore head are massaged gently. *Sweda karma* should be repeated after the *nasya* treatment. The process of *nasya* can be repeated twice or thrice if necessity demands. This process should be repeated for seven days.

Types of Nasya

Generally *Nasya* uses medicated powders and medicated oils. Both these classes can be utilized for the three following types of *nasyas.*

- **Shodhana Nasya** is used to promote secretions which help remove ama from the nose and head. In this treatment, herbs which are hot, pungent and dry are used which eliminates headaches, heaviness in the head, nasal congestion etc.
- **Shamana Nasya** which is palliative and nourishing helps reduce the symptoms, but does not heal the cause of the condition. It offers immediate relief and controls sneezing and nose bleeds.
- **Brumhana Nasya** which is nourishing improves sensory functioning and is good for degenerative brain conditions like epilepsy, mental retardation, Alzheimer's disease etc.

Nasya is divided into *marsha* and *pratimarsha nasya* depending upon the dose of herbal oil applied into the nostrils. The dose of *marsha nasya* is heavier and varies from six to ten drops depending upon the severity of the disease. The dose of *pratimarsha nasya* is two to three drops in each nostril.

4.6.4 *Vasti (Therapeutic Enema)*

Vasti therapy is considered as the most powerful among Panchakarma procedures. The literal meaning of *vasti* is bladder, because centuries ago urinary bladders of animals like cows or buffaloes were filled with medicated liquids and used for enema. *Vasti* is introduction of medicated liquids into the colon through the rectum[17]. The bladders now have been replaced with modern equipment.

Vasti directly affects the colon with its impact on all the *doshas* and *dhatus*. After applying a series of *Vastis*, the toxins in the various tissues are eliminated resulting

in the equilibrium of the *doshas*. *Vasti* is effective for treating kidney stones, spleen disorders, chronic constipation, arthritis and other diseases due to *vata* disorders.

Types of Vasti

Vasti in which herbal oil is applied is called *Annuvasana Vasti*. *Vasti* which uses herbal decoction is called *Nirooha Vasti*. During treatment, both *Annuvasana Vasti* and *Nirooha Vasti* are administrated alternately for specific periods depending upon the severity of the disease and the patient's body constitution.

Vasti Therapy Procedure

Like other Panchakarma procedures, here also preparatory oil and sweat therapies are applied. After this, suitable *Vasti* liquid is injected into the colon through the rectum. In *Annuvasana Vasti*, no harm will occur if the fluid remains inside the colon for long. But in *Nirooha Vasti*, the herbal decoction should be discharged within 45 minutes to one hour. *Nirooha Vasti* stimulates the eliminatory process. *Annuvasana Vasti* nourishes and strengthens the colon. After *Vasti*, the discharged fluid will contain *ama* and other toxins along with faecal matter.

Vasti treatments are classified according to the functions and duration. To achieve certain specific purposes, suitable herbal compounds are prepared. These are added with the basic *vasti* fluids used for *Annuvasana* and *Nirooha*.

i. Vasti Classified by Functions

a) Shodhana Vasti

It cleanses and detoxifies ama by penetrating to the deeper *dhatus*. Here the decoction is prepared with herbs which act as purging agents. *Nirooha* is a prime example of this form of therapy.

b) Lekhana Vasti

Lekhana Vasti is stronger in its effects and is larger in volume when compared to *Shodhana Vasti*. It is useful for *kapha* and *medadhathu* disorders like obesity where excess fatty substances are accumulated and needs to be eliminated.

c) Shamana Vasti

Shamana Vasti is palliative in nature. It contains drugs which reduces problems like rectal bleeding and dysentery.

d) Brumhana Vasti

In *Brumhana Vasti* herbs which nourish and strengthen the *dhatus* are used. Substances like honey, ghee, herbal decoctions using milk, meat, bone marrow etc with rich nutritional value are used for *brumhana vasti*. Most of the *Annuvasana vastis* carry out this function.

e) Rasayana Vasti

Rasayana Vasti rejuvenates and helps strengthening of either specific *dhatus* or the whole body. Fluids containing herbs like *ashvagandha* and *shatavari* are used in this type of *vasti*.

f) Vajeelarana Vasti

Vajeekarana Vasti treats infertility and promotes sexual vitality and vigour. Aphrodisiac and rejuvenating herbs are used in this type of *vasti*.

ii. Vasti Classified by Quantity of Vasti Liquid

a) Mathra Vasti

In *Mathra Vasti*, a small quantity of medicated oil up to a maximum of four ounces is used. No oil or sweat therapies and no diet regulations are necessary. This therapy acts as a good vitalizer and pacifies *vata* aggression

resulting from travel, exercise, stress and excessive sex. This oil *vasti* can be self administered regularly after meals.

b) Sneha Vasti

It is prepared from oleated substances. It is larger and has a greater lubricating effect on both the colon and the body. It has a strong pacifying influence on *vata* and is particularly useful in treating cracking of joints.

c) Kashaya Vasti

When *vasti* is used with more *kwatha* (medicated decoction) then it is called *Kashya Vasti*. Here more than one litre of medicated decoction is applied into the rectum of the patient *Kashya vasti* should always be done after purifying the patient by *virechana* and *vamana*. It should always be done in empty stomach. This treatment is good for treating constipation, obstruction of semen, loss of strength, loss of sensations of organs, chronic rheumatic complaints etc.

d) Uthara Vasti

In *Uthara Vasti,* medicated oil is applied through the vagina and cervix in females and through penis and urethra in males. This treatment is used for certain diseases of the uro-genital tract and urinary organs.

iii. Vasti Classified by Frequency and Duration of Treatment

Charaka classified *vasti* into three types based on the frequency and duration of treatment.

a) Karma Vasti

Karma vasti is a 30-days treatment which is given to people who have acute *vata* disorders. This therapeutic enema begins with two days of *Annuvasanas,* followed by the *Niroohas* that alternates with the *Annuvasanas* for the

next twenty three days. Five more *Annuvasanas* are given during the last five days. Totally eighteen *Annuvasanas* and twelve *Niroohas* are adminstered during this month long treatment.

b) Kala Vasti

Kala Vasti is a fifteen day treatment and is used for patients with *pitta*-dominant constitution and *vata* disorders. During the first twelve days of treatment, *Annuvasana* and *NiroohaVastis* are given alternately; *Annuvasana* is given repeatedly in the last three days of treatment. During the fifteen days treatment, nine *Annuvasana vastis* and six *Nirooha vastis* will be administered to the patient.

c) Yoga Vasti

Yoga *Vasti* is an eight day treatment prescribed to patients of *Kapha* constitution with *Vata* disorders. The treatment begins with an *Annuvasana,* alternates with three *Niroohas* and concludes with two *Annuvasanas*.

4.6.5 Raktamokshana (bloodletting)

Susruta, the father of Ayurvedic surgery combined the two types of *vastis—Annuasana* and *Nirooha* discussed by *Charaka* into one category and added *Rakthamokshana* as the fifth procedure in the Panchakarma therapy. According to him certain diseases are caused by vitiation of blood[18]. This can be effectively treated by letting out the vitiated blood. So he devised the therapeutic withdrawal of blood through surgical venesection called *Raktamokshana*.

Sushruta noted that when ama or toxins are collected, it circulates throughout the body with blood. He framed *raktamokshana* as a purification treatment to be used when excess toxins are being carried in the blood to the periphery of the body. *Raktamokshana* is carried out with the help of precise surgical instrument. Another method is to suck blood from a slight cut made on the surface of the affected part with the help of an instrument made of the horn of

a cow or a buffalo. Leeching, selective biting by leeches on affected parts is also used in certain cases. Sterile syringes are also used nowadays.

Blood letting is used to treat blood related diseases including skin disorders, chronic itching, headaches, eczema, leukoderma and hypertension. Children, pregnant women, the aged, anaemic people and those suffering from leukaemia and liver cirrhosis should not undergo this treatment. *Snehana* and *Swedana* therapies do not precede bloodletting. *Raktamokshan*a is the most limited among the five *Panchakarma* procedures.

Leeching – A Raktamokshana Procedure

Biting of leeches on affected parts of the body to remove vitiated blood is called leeching. Firstly, the area where the leech is to bite is cleaned and dried. Then, a drop of milk is applied on the affected area or a small cut is made after which the leech is placed on it. The milk or blood will induce the leech to bite in to the flesh and suck out vitiated blood from the diseased part. After sufficient quantity of the unclean blood has been drained out, a little powdered salt or honey is applied to the mouth of the leech so that it withdraws. The wound is then washed with cold water.

Non-poisonous leeches are used for leeching. The leeches used for treatment are usually kept in a pot or a little tank filled with mud and pond water and fed adequately. Leeching is practiced in Kerala.

4.7 Other Important Treatments in Kerala

The Ayurveda texts describe another set of treatments which are applied extremely in localized areas of the body. Even though they are not introduced in to the body, they are still called *Vasti* because the medicated substances are retained in specific areas of the body for a period of time. They are the following:

4.7.1 *Shirovasti*

Shirovasti is the process of allowing medicated oil to remain on the head for a prescribed time, usually up to 45 minutes. Here special herbal oils are poured in a cap fitted mainly on the shaven head. The patient must be subjected to oleation and sudation therapies before *shirovasti.* A specially made round leather cap without top is attached to the head. The oil which is made lukewarm must be poured in to this apparatus till it rises and remains at a level of 3 to 4 inches above the top of the skull. This process can be continued for 7 days till mucous discharge oozes out of the mouth, eyes and nose of the patient, which shows completion of treatment. After removing the oil inside the cap and further wiping the head, fresh oil is again applied to the head, neck and the body and the patient is given body bath in medicated water. Head bath is forbidden during the course of treatment. *Shirovasti* is extremely useful for treating diseases like vascular headaches, cataract, memory loss, insanity, sinus headaches schizophrenia and facial paralysis. The application of *shirovasti* treatment is shown in figure 4.5.

Figure 4.5 The application of shirovasti treatment

Source : Ayurvedic Health Holidays in Kerala, Brochure by Department of Tourism, Kerala.

4.7.2 Urovasti

Urovasti is administered on the *uras* or chest. In this treatment a container is made on the chest using black gram dough and medicated oil is poured into it and kept there for a specific time. It reduces pain in the sternum area and strengthens the heart.

4.7.3 *Kativasti*

In *Kativasti,* oil is poured into a container of black gram dough made on the lower back portion of the body and kept there for a specified time. This benefits muscle spasm and rigidity of the lower spine and strengthens the bone tissue in that area.

4.7.4 *Netravasti (Netra tarpana)*

In *Netravasti,* medicated ghee is applied to the eyes. The ghee is kept in a dam constructed around the eye sockets, made of the dough from black gram flour. After this the patient opens and closes his eyes intermittently for a maximum of five minutes. This treatment is nourishing for the eyes, removes eye strain and improves vision. It is recommended for treating ailments like glaucoma and night blindness.

Various special treatments meant for controlling various diseases and rejuvenating the body is also in practice in Kerala. These special treatments are mentioned below.

4.7.5 *Udwartana*

In *Udwartana,* the patient is massaged with medicinal oils or with dried, finely pulverized herbal powder (*churna*). The oily massage with dried herbal powder is effective for treating obesity, rheumatoid arthritis and many *kapha* disorders. The speciality of this therapy is that the stroking motion during the massage is upwards or towards the heart.

4.7.6 *Talam*

Application of medicated paste on the crown of the head is called *Talam*. *Talams* are of various types according to the nature of the ailment. *Talam* precedes treatments like *Pizhichil, Navarakizhi* and *Sarvangadhara*.

4.7.7 *Lepana*

External application of medicated paste on the affected part of the body is known as *Lepana*. *Lepana* is recommended in several types of pains associated with inflammatory conditions. Ingredients of the paste vary according to the nature of the ailment.

4.7.8 *Sirolepanam*

Sirolepanam, literally means covering of the head. The crown is kept covered with gooseberry paste for a specific time. Gooseberries, from which the seeds have been removed, are soaked in a mixture of buttermilk and medicinal decoction to prepare the medicinal paste. This is then stored in earthen vessels overnight. A paste is made from the soaked gooseberries next day to be used for application on the patient's body.

The patient has to get his head shaven before undergoing treatment. A headband is tied on and then oil is applied on the head of the seated patient. After this, enough gooseberry paste is applied all over the head. The paste is kept on for a prescribed time.

A second dose is applied and kept for a while after removing the first dose. After removing the second dose, oil is applied on the head and then a bath is to be taken using water boiled with *Amalaki* fruits or with some other herbs suited to the condition of the person. *Sirolepanam* is effective for treating *vata* disorders like facial paralysis, hemiplegia and so on.

4.7.9 *Karnapoorana*

Karnapoorana is a process in which medicated oil is applied to the ears for 5 to 10 minutes. In this treatment, the patient is made to lie down on one side and lukewarm, purified and medicated oil prescribed according to the illness, is gently poured into the ear. After remaining in the same position for about five minutes, the patient turns

and then oil is applied to the other ear also. In severe cases, the process is repeated for a week or more. This process helps to clean the ear and avoid ailments like ear infections and deafness.

4.7.10 *Chavutti Pizhichil (Oil Bath)*

This is the most complicated among all massages. The masseur literally hangs from the ceiling by hooks and carries out the massage with the soles of his or her feet. The purpose of this massage is to apply the pressure of the masseur's body very selectively in appropriate nerve centres (*marma*) and in the tissues and musculoskeletal structure of the patient. This form of massage allows the therapist to vary the pressure and reach over the patient. It is used for patients who need to condition their bodies for high performance or those with acute problems in the nervous system, but not for paralysis or stroke victims.

4.8 Rules to be Strictly Followed During Ayurvedic Treatment

The following rules shall be carefully followed by the patients during ayurvedic treatment.

- Strictly follow the diet regimen.
- Strictly follow *Brahmacharya,* i.e. stay away from sexual relations.
- Avoid sleep during daytime.
- Never restrict excretion.
- Drink boiled water.
- Avoid travelling which cause too much jerking.
- Keep away body from snow, heat and rain.
- Speaking in a medium voice avoiding exertion.
- Avoid sitting in same position for a long time and avoid walking through steps.

- Avoid drinking and smoking.
- Keeping the mind in peace.
- Avoiding anger and sadness.
- Concentrating the mind in prayers

Various special treatments are widely practiced in Kerala. Therapies like *Pizhichil, Kizhi, Dhara, Shirovasti, Lepana, Pichu, Talam* etc. were developed by the renowned ayurvedic scholars of Kerala. All these treatments have excellent clinical effect.

4.9 Disease Management in Ayurveda

According to Ayurveda, illness is caused by the imbalance of the *doshas* (humors). So medicines derived from various sources of nature are used not only to treat a particular disease, but to restore complete harmony of the body.

In Ayurveda, various medicinal preparations are prepared from the substances collected from three sources:

- Animal Sources
- Vegetable Sources
- Mineral Sources

From animal sources, substances like honey, milk & milk products, fat, bile, bone, bone marrow, horn, blood, flesh, semen, urine and so on are obtained and used for preparations of ayurvedic medicines. Various flowers, roots, bark, plants, leaves, fruits etc which are a part of vegetable sources are also used. Various minerals like Gold, silver, iron, lead, tin and their oxides, arsenous sulphide, arsenous disulphide, salt, calcium, antimony etc are also used for preparation of medicines. These various substances (*dravyas*) from various sources are purified before they are used for preparations of drugs. Sushrutha has classified all the drugs into six categories on the basis of their main characteristics. They are *Madhura Varga*

(sweet), *Amla Varga* (sour), *Lavana Varga* (salty), *Katu Varga* (pungent), *Tikta Varga* (bitter) and *Kashaya Varga* (astringent). Medicines in Ayurveda are termed as *Oushadams*.

4.10 Ayurvedic Medicinal Preparations

In Ayurveda, the disease management is in two ways: by following diet regimen *(padhyam)* and through medicines *(oushadhams)*. Medicines are used in *Shamana* and *Shodhana* therapies. In Panchakarma too, which is a *Shodhana* theraphy, medicinal preparations are used. Various medicinal preparations are as follows[19].

- **Sevya**—A *thaila* (medicated oil) that is taken internally is called a *Sevya*. Here, the base is either gingelly oil or castor oil.
- **Kuzhambu**— This is made by adding the medicinal element to suitable base oil which can be castor oil or ghee. This is a speciality of Kerala.
- **Ghruta**—*Ghruta* is prepared by heating ghee with the prescribed quantity of the decoction and the fine paste of the drug as specified in the formula. *Ghruta* is used in *Snehana* process; which is a preparatory procedure for Panchakarma.
- **Asava**—*Asavas* are made by adding powdered medicine, raisins, jaggery and *thathiripoo*, a flower that acts as a fermenting agent, to water that has boiled and cooled. The mixture is stored in earthen pots for around 30 days for fermentation and sedimentation, ghee fluid obtained after removing the sediment is used for treatment. There is no expiry date for fermented products like *asava*. Their potency increases with time.
- **Swarasa (Extract)**—The medicinal substance from which extract is to be taken should be fresh and juicy. It is cut into small pieces and sometimes slightly crushed. Then with the help of a squeezer,

the *swarasa* or extract is taken. Substances from which extract cannot be squeezed should be cut into small pieces, crushed, and then a paste prepared. This paste is then squeezed for the extract.

- **Kvatha (Kashaya or Decoction)**—*Kashaya* means decoction or extract. In *Kashaya,* drugs in their raw form are cut into small pieces, crushed and then boiled in water in an earthen vessel till the volume is reduced to a quarter. The decoction thus obtained is filtered and honey, sugar, jaggery etc. are added if required. There are more than thousand kinds of *Kashayas*.
- **Sitakashaya**—Crushed medicinal substances are steeped in water in a closed vessel for twelve hours. Water that has been boiled and cooled or clean rain water can be used. After the stipulated time, the contents are passed through a filter and the liquid thus obtained is the *Sitakashaya*.
- **Phanta Kashaya**—Here a medicinal substance is crushed and mixed with water and then the mixture sieved to obtain *Phantakashaya*.
- **Churna (Powder)**—Here, medicinal substances mentioned in the formula are cleaned, dried and crushed to become fine powder. The powder is then sifted with a piece of fine cloth or a new sieve with fine meshes. The grains left on the sieve can further be crushed and sifted to obtain more powder.
- **Kalka (Paste)** —The medicinal substances are cut into pieces and crushed. While adding water, it is then ground on a stone to get a paste of thick consistency. In some cases, other liquids are used.
- **Lehya**—The *Lehya* which is of semi-solid form is made by mixing *Kashaya, Swarasa,* water and a sweetening element like jaggery over a fire until

they are blended well. It is left to cool and then honey, ghee and oil are added to obtain *Lehya*. In some cases, *Lehya* will be ready for use before adding honey, ghee and oil.

- **Thaila**—Adding medicinal elements to an oil base, usually gingelly oil makes a thaila. *Thailas* can be applied externally or taken internally. The potency of a *thaila* is improved by adding more and more ingredients every day over a fixed period of time. For preparing it, fine paste of drug is mixed with oil, boiled, stirred continuously and strained.
- **Arishta**—*Arishtas* can be made by adding sweetening elements like sugar, jaggery, honey and *churna* to *kashayas*. The mixture is kept sealed in earthen pots for thirty days. The porosity of the earthen pots helps maintain temperature of around twenty seven degrees inside which facilitates fermentation. Its potency increases with time.
- **Gulika**—Medicines in the form of tablets or pills are known as *gulikas*. Medicinal paste is first rolled into small ball and dried in the sunlight to make *gulikas*.
- **Vadaka**—*Vadakas* are also made like *gulikas*, but are bigger in size.
- **Anjana**—These are medications for eye diseases.
- **Kshara**—*Ksharas* are alkaline substances obtained from raw drugs by burning them. The ash obtained is dissolved in water, strained and evaporated to make it dry.
- **Bhasma**—A powdered form of a substance obtained by calcinations of metals, minerals or animal products, by a special process in closed crucibles or in pits covered with cow dung cakes is known as *bhasma*.

These various medicinal preparations are widely used for various Ayurvedic treatments in Kerala.

4.11 Availability of Human Resources and Medical Facilities

Kerala is one of the states which has introduced dedicated Ayurvedic treatment to people at various levels. Ayurvedic hospitals at various levels are available in Kerala. Primary Health Centres, taluk hospitals, district hospitals and Ayurveda Colleges, offers a range of services to patients. The doctors coming out of various Ayurveda colleges act as a corner stone of Kerala's ayurvedic system. Ayurveda colleges include some very old colleges started long ago. These colleges offer B.A.M.S. course and other higher courses.

In 1970, the Central Government started the 'Central Council of Indian Medicine"(CCIM) and BAMS Course was introduced under it with effect from 1971. Dedicated ayurvedic treatment is offered in Kerala by the following hospitals which are shown in table 4.1.

Table 4.1

Ayurvedic Hospitals in Kerala

Ayurveda Colleges	5
Ayurveda Hospitals	111
Ayurveda Dispensaries	631
Private Ayurveda Hospitals	4922

Source: Brilliants Year Book, 2002 and Manorama Year Book 1999.

Medical and treatment facilities in Kerala are equivalent to that of developed western countries and are comparatively superior to other states of India. Here, Ayurveda's contribution is significant. The details are given in table 4.2.

Table 4.2

Health Scenario in Kerala

Health Factors	*Kerala*	*India*
General mortality rate (per 1000)	6.40	8.50
Infant mortality rate (per 1000)	12	58
Birth rate (Per 1000)	17.90	25.80
Life Expectancy—Men	71.70	64.10
Life Expectancy—women	75	65.40
Per capita income	Rs. 29601	Rs. 25825
Number of Medical colleges	40	——
Births with trained assistance	97.70	42.80
Child immunization	81.20	54.40

Source: Kerala—Performance, Facts and Ffigures, Pearson Education 2006-07.

Ayurveda is having a significant role in maintaining the general health of the people of Kerala. When compared to other indigenous medicinal systems, Ayurveda's contribution is significant. The number of registered medical practitioners is given in Table 4.3.

Table 4.3

Registered Medical Practitioners in Kerala

Allopathy	24,883
Homeopathy	7,253
Ayurveda	13,329
Siddha	1,379
Unani	59
Total	46,903

Source: Manorama Year Book 1999.

Kerala with its long history of Ayurvedic treatment offered to the mankind, some unique treatment methods which are rejuvenative as well as curative. Ayurveda has helped the state in achieving excellent health standards. It is also helping the state exchequer by gaining valuable foreign exchange.

References

1. Franklyn, V. (2002); *God's Own Medicine,* An Economic Times special report, Mumbai, p. 3.
2. Thirumulpad, Vaidyabhooshanam, Raghavan (2002); *Ashtavaidyanmar,* Mathrubhoomi Arogyamasika (Malayalam), Kozhikode, p. 20.
3. Franklyn. V (2002); *God's Own Medicine,* An Economic Times special report, Mumbai, p. 3.
4. Namboothiri Vaidyamadom, Cheriya, Narayanan (2002); *Rasayanchikitsa,* Mathrubhoomi Arogyamasika (Malayalam), p. 69.
5. *Ibid.,* p. 69.
6. Joshi, Sunil V. (1998); *Ayurveda & Panchakarma,* Motilal Banarssidass Publishers, New Delhi, p. 203.
7. Mahadevan. L. (2002); *Panchakarma,* Compendium of Invited Lectures, World Ayurveda Congress, Kochi, p. 78.
8. Joshi, Sunil. V (1998); *Ayurveda & Panchakarma,* Motilal Banarssidass Publishers, New Delhi, p. 180.
9. Varrier, Krishna, P.K. Sharma, Subramanya S. (1982); *Keraleeyachikitsa,* Vasudeva Vilasom Pharmacy, Thiruvananthapuram, p. 30.
10. Vinodkumar, G., (2002); *Kerala specialties in Panchakarma,* Souvenir, World Ayurveda Congress, Kochi, p. 55.
11. Varrier, Krishna. P. K., Sharma, Subramanya. S. (1982); *Keraleeyachikitsa,* Vasudeva Vilasom Pharmacy, Thiruvananthapuram, p. 8.
12. *Ibid.,* p. 26.

13. Vinodkumar, G. (2002); *Kerala Specialties in Panchakarma*, Compendium of invited Lectures, World Ayurveda Congress, Kochi, p. 55.

14. Lad, Vasant (2002); *An Introduction to Panchakarma*, Science India, Thiruvananthapuram, p. 42.

15. *Ibid*., p. 44.

16. Joshi, Sunil V. (1998); *Ayurveda & Panchakarma*, Motilal Banarssidass Publishers, New Delhi, p. 212.

17. *Ibid*., p. 225.

18. Lad, Vasant (2002); *An Introduction to Panchakarma*, Science India, Thiruvananthapuram, p. 44.

19. *Ayurveda—The Mantra of Niramaya* (2002); Compact Disc, Department of Tourism, Thiruvananthapuram, Kerala.

5

Ayurvedic Tourism: Socio-economic Impacts and the Importance of Marketing

This chapter presents an empirical analysis of data with regard to the scores analysed in connection with the study on Ayurvedic tourism. The data used for the study was collected on the basis of a questionnaire. The respondents were asked to give their views on a number of aspects related to Ayurvedic tourism in Kerala. The survey was conducted at various Ayurvedic centers including Ayurvedic hospitals, resorts and hotels where Ayurvedic treatments are offered to tourists. The following statistical methods were used to analyse the data.

5.1 CATPCA—Principal Components Analysis for Categorical Data

This procedure simultaneously quantifies categorical variables while reducing the dimensionality of the data. Categorical principal components analysis is also known

by the acronym CATPCA, for categorical principal components analysis.

The goal of principal components analysis is to reduce an original set of variables into a smaller set of uncorrelated components that represent most of the information found in the original variables. The technique is most useful when a large number of variables prohibit effective interpretation of the relationships between objects (subjects and units). By reducing the dimensionality, you interpret a few components rather than a large number of variables.

Standard principal components analysis assumes linear relationships between numeric variables. On the other hand, the optimal-scaling approach allows variables to be scaled at different levels. Categorical variables are optimally quantified in the specified dimensionality. As a result, non linear relationships between variables can be modelled.

5.2 Method of Least Square

Given a set of data points, often called "observations," a common need is to condense the data by fitting it to a model in the form of a parametric equation. This "model equation" can be anything that the user desires — it can range from a simple polynomial to an extremely complex model with many parameters. One important consideration in selecting an appropriate model is the underlying law that the data represents. Optimally, the model should be chosen to reflect that law so that the parameters in the curve fit have physical interpretation and meaning.

Data modelling may be performed by several techniques: interpolation, regression, or data smoothing. Interpolation and regression are the types supported by Curve Expert. Interpolation guarantees that the fitted curve will pass through each and every data point. Regression simply ensures that the "merit function", which is an arbitrary function that measures the disagreement between the data and the model, is minimized. In this approach,

the model parameters are adjusted until the merit function becomes as small as possible. One of the features of Curve Expert is the large number of non linear regression models that are available. This type of model is the most commonly used in real-world applications.

One of the features of the Curve Expert is the availability of a large number of non-linear regression models. From these models, in order to find the best model to be fitted, we consider the coefficient of determination R^2, which shows the percentage of total variation of the dependent variable that can be explained by independent variables.

5.3 Principal Components Analysis for the Scores of Inadequate Quality of Services in Ayurvedic Centres

A variety of factors directly related to Ayurvedic tourism were analyzed. In this assignment, we examined 30 Ayurvedic centers located across Kerala and asked questions to entrepreneurs, doctors and visitors on the following aspects. In this survey, we interviewed around 200 personnel and whatever replies we have received have been depicted through statistical tools called CATPCA and Method of Least Square. The factors considered for the study here are the following.

- Whether the Ayurvedic centers are offering medicines and treatment of right quality to tourists.
- Whether the centers have adequate treatment space and utensils for treatment.
- Whether the centers have well qualified and trained doctors and masseurs.
- Whether the Ayurvedic centers are following traditional Ayurvedic methods in true spirit.
- Whether the duration of Ayurvedic treatments is as per Ayurvedic rules.

Table 5.1

Principal Components Analysis for the Scores of Inadequate Quality of Services in Ayurvedic Centres

Correlations Transformed Variables

	Right quality of medicines & treatment	*Treatment space & utensils*	*Well qualified doctors*	*Trained masseurs*	*Traditional Ayurvedic methods*	*Definition as per Ayurvedic rules*
Right quality of medicines & treatment	1.000	.501	.191	.446	.525	.662
Treatment space & utensils	.501	1.000	-.044	.885	.978	.103
Well qualified doctors	.191	-.044	1.000	-.008	-.019	.488
Trained masseurs	.446	.885	-.008	1.000	.797	.126
Traditional Ayuervedic methods	.525	.978	-.019	.797	1.000	.155
Duration as per Ayurvedic rules	.662	.103	.488	.126	.155	1.000
Dimension	1	2	3	4	5	6
Eigen value	3.225	1.670	.676	.231	.193	.006

Source: Field survey at Ayurvedic Centres.

The data represented in the above Table 5.1 is a result of conversion of multivariable original data into a set of uncorrelated mean, which quantifies and compresses multivariable into a single data. For the factors considered here, we have taken a mean for different variables that are being drawn in x as well as y-axis. Taking an example of the first factor ie, right quality of medicines and treatment, the author has taken a mean of multivariables like very low, low, average, high and very high as 1.000 for x as well as y axis as the mean of responses for the above mentioned variables. .501 is the result of correlation between the factors, right quality of medicines and treatment with the other factor treatment space and utensils. This method is followed for all other factors. Here we are considering variables like right quality of medicines and treatment, adequate treatment space and utensils, well-qualified doctors, trained masseurs, traditional Ayurvedic methods and duration as per Ayurvedic rules. By using the above statistics, we get the following object scores table through various statistical methods like frequencies, modes etc. By using the various variables, we get the following objective scores and objective plots which are shown in Table 5.2.

Table 5.2

Object Scores for Variable, Inadequate Quality of Services

Variable principal normalization

	Dimension 1	Dimension 2
1	-.917	-.775
2	-.917	-.775
3	-.222	2.498
4	-.844	-.041

5	-.338	-.637
6	1.832	-1.271
7	-.595	-.879
8	-.283	.025
9	2.448	.162
10	-.844	-.041
11	1.166	.921
12	-.123	-.067
13	-.242	-.477
14	-.023	1.052
15	1.962	-1.185
16	-.558	-.287
17	-.588	.200
18	.286	2.328
19	-.283	.025
20	-.917	-.775

Source: Field survey at Ayurvedic centres.

In table 5.2, the object points are concentrated between 1 and 0. Hence we can arrive at a conclusion that most of the Ayurvedic centers are not providing adequate quality of services. A graphical representation of the inadequate quality of services and facilities in Ayurvedic centers based on object points received as a result of the study is shown below in graph 5.1.

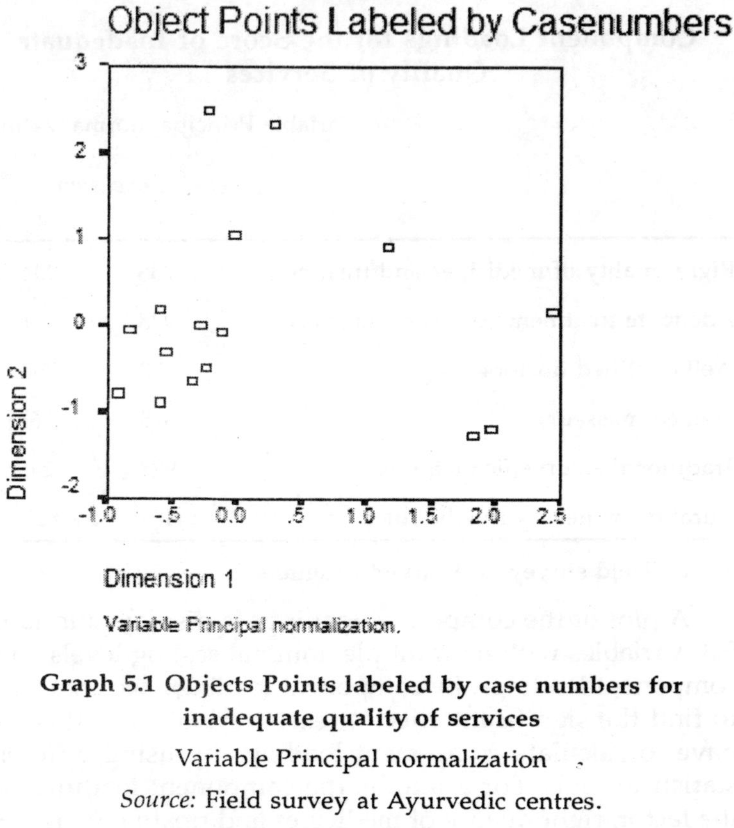

Graph 5.1 Objects Points labeled by case numbers for inadequate quality of services

Variable Principal normalization

Source: Field survey at Ayurvedic centres.

In the above graph, points are concentrated between -1 and 0. So we arrive at a conclusion that most of the Ayurvedic centers are not providing adequate quality of services. Factors like use of right quality of medicines and treatment, availability of adequate treatment space and utensils, presence of well qualified doctors and masseurs, adoption of traditional Ayurvedic methods and proper duration of treatments were considered to arrive at this conclusion.

Table 5.3
Component Loadings for the Score of Inadequate Quality of Services

Variable Principal normalization.

	Dimension 1	2
Right quality of medicines and treatment	.736	.434
Adequate treatment space and utensils	.938	-.306
Well qualified doctors	.122	.758
Trained masseurs	.875	-.262
Traditional Ayurvedic methods	.927	-.248
Duration as per Ayurvedic rules	.404	.827

Source: Field survey at Ayurvedic Centers.

A plot of the component loadings is displayed in table 5.3. Variables with no multiple nominal scaling levels have component loadings. By component loadings, we are trying to find the significant effect of each variable. For this, we have to calculate component loadings by using different statistical tools. For example, the component loadings for the factor, right quality of medicines and treatment are .736 in dimension 1 and .434 in dimension 2. This method follows for the other factor too. For pictorial representation, we need the two dimensional components which is displayed in the above table. The contribution of various factors analysed for study towards the overall performance is shown above. A graphical representation of the contribution of various factors towards the overall performance and the results are shown below in Graph 5.2.

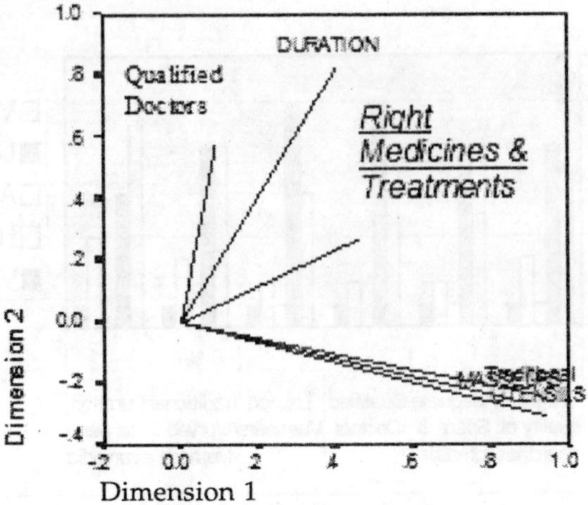

Variable Principal normalization

Graph 5.2 Component Loadings for inadequate quality of services

Source: Field survey at Ayurvedic centers.

From the above graph, we can conclude that adoption of traditional Ayurvedic methods, availability of adequate treatment space and utensils, presence of trained masseurs give the same contribution to the overall performance. The effect of presence of qualified doctors, duration of treatments as per Ayurvedic rules, use of right quality of medicines and treatment has the contribution entirely different from other factors.

Table 5.4. Percentage analysis for Scores of Inadequate Quality of Services

	Right quality of medicines	*Treatment space & utensils*	*Well qualified doctors*	*Trained Masseurs*	*Traditional Ayurvedic methods*	*Duration as per Ayurvedic rules*
Very Low	35.0%	40.0%	35.0%	30.0%	40.0%	45.0%
Low	40.0%	40.0%	50.0%	50.0%	40.0%	30.0%
Average	5.0%	5.0%		5.0%		
High	15.0%	10.0%	10.0%	10.0%	15.0%	20.0%
Very High	5.0%	5.0%	5.0%	5.0%	5.0%	5.0%

Source: Field survey at Ayurvedic centers.

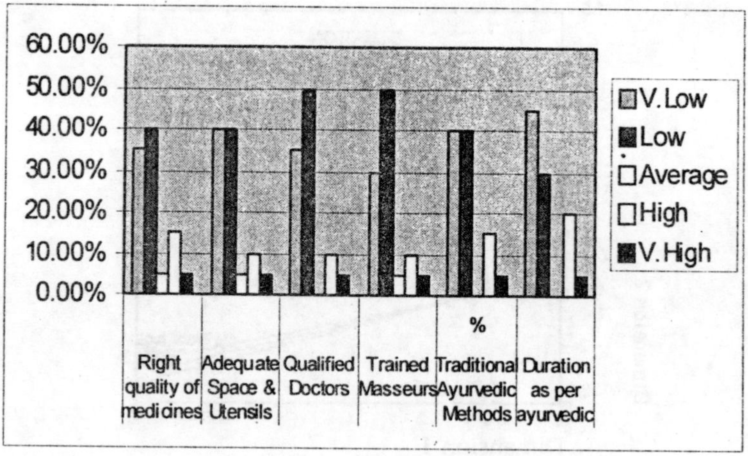

Graph 5.3 Scores of Inadequate Quality of Services.

Source: Field survey at Ayurvedic centers.

Respondents were asked to give their views regarding the above factors related to inadequate quality of services at Ayurvedic centers. The responses proved that the overall quality of services and facilities offered at majority of Ayurvedic centers as inadequate. A graphical representation of the responses is shown in graph 5.3. The graph shows that the quality of services in the Ayurvedic sector is highly inadequate.

5.4 Principal Components Analysis for the Scores of Obstacles in the Field of Ayurvedic Tourism Development

A variety of factors related to obstacles in the field of tourism was analyzed. The study analyzed the following factors.

- Whether the commercialization of *Ayurveda* has resulted in lessening the quality of medicines.
- The perception of Ayurvedic doctors about the feasibility of involvement of tourism in the growth of *Ayurveda*.
- Whether the tourists are willing to stay in treatment centers for adequate period.
- Difficulties from the part of tourists in properly discharging the treatment.
- Whether bad reputation of Ayurvedic centers affects tourist arrivals to Kerala.
- Whether Ayurvedic tourism development has resulted in the services becoming unavailable to the local population.
- Whether Ayurvedic tourism development has resulted in the depletion of herbal wealth of Kerala.
- Whether fast growth and modernisation has resulted in deteriorating the quality of medicines.
- Whether the clients are strictly following the diet regimen during treatment.

The data represented in the above Table 5.5 is a result of conversion of multivariable original data into a set of uncorrelated mean, which quantifies and compresses multivariable into a single data. For the factors considered here, we have taken a mean for different variables that are being drawn in x as well as y-axis. Taking an example of the first factor ie, commercialization of Ayurveda, the author has taken a mean of multivariable like very low, low, average, high and very high as 1.000 for x as well as y axis as the mean of responses for the above mentioned variables. -.213 is the result of correlation between the factor, commercialization of Ayurveda with the other factor, growth of Ayurveda. This method is followed for all other factors. Here we are considering variables like

Table 5.5: Principal Component Analysis for the Scores of Obstacles in the Field of Ayurvedic Tourism Development in Kerala

Correlations Transformed Variables *(Source: Field Survey at Ayurvedic Centers)*

	Commercialization of Ayurveda	*Growth of Ayurveda*	*Adequate Period*	*Difficulties from tourists*	*Bad Reputation of centers*	*Service unavailability to local*	*Depletion of Herbal wealth*	*Reduction in Quality of Ayurveda*	*Proper diet regimen*
Commercialisation of ayurverda	1.000	-.213	-.174	-.129	.343	-.477	-.291	-.003	.165
Growth of *Ayurveda*	-.213	1.000	-.080	.712	-.354	-.363	.769	.678	.093
Adequate Period	-.174	-.080	1.000	-.133	-.536	.144	-.127	-.026	-.990
Difficulties from Tourists	-.129	.712	-.133	1.000	-.165	-.285	.529	.479	.129
Bad Reputation of Centers	.343	-.354	-.536	-.165	1.000	-.170	-.208	-.539	.533
Service unavailability to local People	-.477	-.363	.144	-.285	-.170	1.000	-.236	-.192	-.148
Depletion of Wealth	-.291	.769	-.127	.529	-.208	-.236	1.000	.559	.134
Reduction in Quality of Medicines	-.003	.678	-.026	.479	-.539	-.192	.559	1.000	.016
Proper Diet regimen	.165	.093	-.990	.129	.533	-.148	.134	.016	1.000
Dimension	1	2	3	4	5	6	7	8	9
Eigen value	3.216	2.603	1.355	.724	.480	.318	.155	.140	.010

commercialization of Ayurveda, results of involvement of tourism for the growth of Ayurveda, willingness of tourists to stay in treatment centers for adequate period, difficulties from the part of tourists, bad reputation of Ayurvedic centers and its impact on tourist arrivals, impact of growth of Ayurvedic tourism on local population, depletion of herbal wealth of Kerala, impact of modernization on quality of medicines and adherence to diet regimen by tourists. Correlation analysis helps us in determining the degree of relationship between two or more variables. By using the above statistics, we get the following object scores table through various statistical methods like frequencies, modes etc. By using the various variables, we get the following objective scores and objective plots which are shown in Table 5.6.

Table 5.6

Object scores for the variable, Obstacles in the field of Ayurvedic Tourism Development

Variable Principal normalization

	Dimension	
	1	*2*
1	.373	.021
2	.374	.007
3	.549	-.089
4	-3.449	-.321
5	.484	1.154
6	.422	.003
7	.410	.741
8	.639	-.096
9	-.276	.662
10	.515	-.040
11	.239	-3.960
12	.612	.294
13	-2.122	.736

14	.780	.360
15	-.295	.238
16	-.111	-.713
17	.511	.248
18	-.294	.041
19	.363	.700
20	.276	.015

Source: Field Survey at Ayurvedic Centers.

In table 5.6, the object points are concentrated between 0and 1. Hence we can arrive at a conclusion that obstacles exist in the field of Ayurvedic tourism development in Kerala. A graphical representation of the obstacles in the field of Ayurvedic tourism developments in Kerala based on object points received as a result of the study is shown below in graph 5.4.

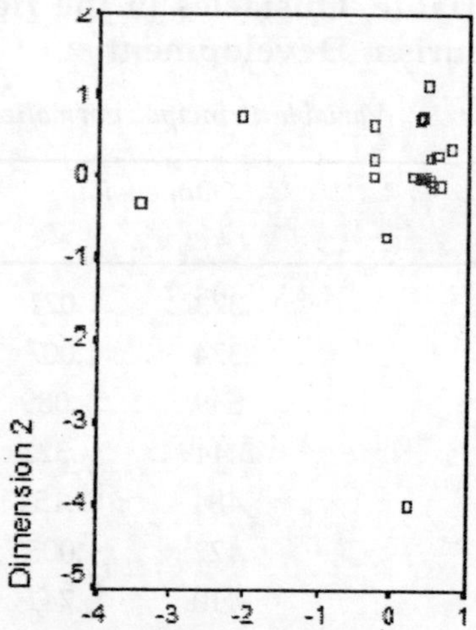

Variable Principal Normalisation

Source: Field survey at Ayurvedic centers

Graph 5.4 Object scores for the variable, Obstacles in the field of Ayurvedic Tourism Development

In the above graph, the object points are concentrated between 0 and 1. So we can arrive at a conclusion that obstacles exists in the Ayurvedic tourism developments of Kerala. For arriving at this conclusion, factors like commercialisation of Ayurveda, results of involvement of tourism for the growth of Ayurveda, willingness of tourists to stay in treatment centers for adequate period, difficulties from the part of tourists, bad reputation of Ayurvedic centers and its result on tourist arrivals, impact of growth of Ayurvedic tourism on local population, depletion of herbal wealth of Kerala, impact of modernisation on quality of medicines, adherence to diet regimen by tourists were considered.

Table 5.7
Component Loadings for scores for Obstacles in the field of Ayurvedic Tourism Development

	Dimension	
	1	2
Commercialization of *Ayurveda*	-.239	-.436
Growth of *Ayurveda*	.940	-.063
Adequate period	-.052	.913
Difficulties from tourists	.773	-.155
Bad Reputation of centers	-.468	-.726
Service unavailable to local people	-.331	.421
Depletion of herbal wealth	.831	-.095
Reduction in quality of medicines	.808	.065
Proper diet regiment	.056	-.912

Variable Principal normalization.

Source : Field Survey at Ayurvedic Centers.

A plot of the component loadings is displayed in table 5.7. Variables with no multiple nominal scaling levels have

component loadings. By component loadings, we are trying to find the significant effect of each variable. For this, we have to calculate component loadings by using different statistical tools. For example, the component loadings for the factor, Commercialization of *Ayurveda* are -.239 in dimension 1 and -.436 in dimension 2. This method follows for the other factors too. For pictorial representation, we need the two dimensional components which is displayed in the above table. The contribution of various factors analyzed for study towards the overall performance is shown above. A graphical representation of the contribution of various factors towards the overall performance and the results are shown below in graph 5.5.

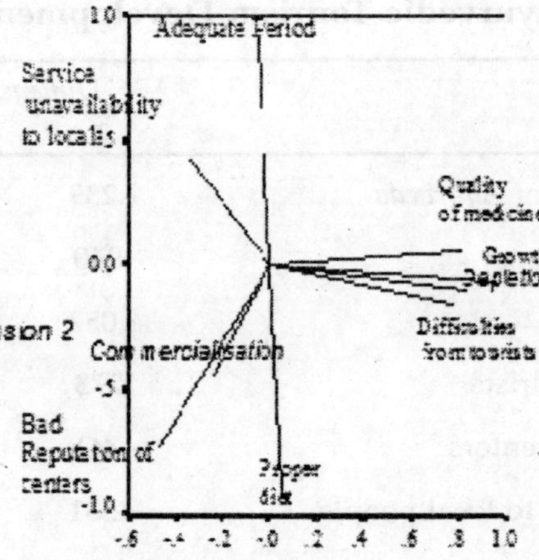

Source: Field survey at Ayurvedic centers

Graph 5.5. Component Loadings for the scores of Obstacles in the field of Ayurvedic Tourism Development

Table 5.8

Percentage Analysis for the Scores of Obstacles in the Field of Ayurvedic Tourism Development

	Commercialization of Ayurveda	*Growth of Ayurveda*	*Adequate Period*	*Dificulties from tourists*	*Bad Reputa- tion of centers*	*Service unavailability to local peiople*	*Depletion of herbal wealth*	*Reduction in quality of medicines*	*Proper diet regimen*
	%			%					
Very Low	10.0%	10.0%	5.0%	20.0%	5.0%	15.0%	15.0%	5.0%	25.0%
Low	25.0%	20.0%	30.0%	25.0%	25.0%	55.0%	50.0%	15.0%	30.0%
Average	5.0%	5.0%			5.0%	10.0%	10.0%	5.0%	
High	45.0%	55.0%	55.0%	50.0%	50.0%	20.0%	25.0%	60.0%	40.0%
Very High	15.0%	10.0%	10.0%	5.0%	15.0%			15.0%	5.0%

Source: Field survey at Ayurvedic centers

The above graph reveals that quality of medicine, growth of *Ayurveda*, herbal wealth, and difficulties from tourists give the same contribution to the overall performance. The effect of bad reputation of centers & commercialization of *Ayurveda* has the same contribution. Proper diet regimen, service unavailability to local people, adequate treatment period has the contribution entirely different from other factors.

Respondents were asked to give their expert views regarding the above factors related to obstacles in the field of Ayurvedic tourism development. The responses proved that there a number of obstacles in the field of Ayurvedic tourism development in Kerala. A graphical representation of the responses is shown below in Graph 5.6.

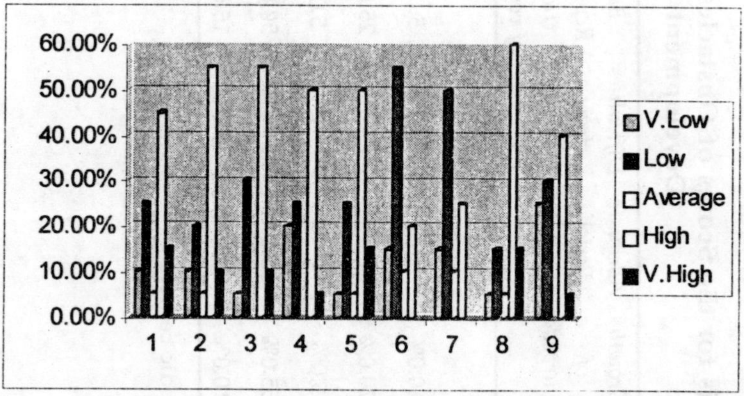

Graph 5.6 Scores of obstacles in the field of Ayurvedic tourism development

Source: Field survey at Ayurvedic centers

The above graph shows that there are a number of obstacles in the field of Ayurvedic tourism development in Kerala.

5.5 Principal Components Analysis for the Scores of Scope of Ayurvedic Tourism

A number of factors related to scope of Ayurvedic tourism were analysed. The factors considered for study are the following:

- Whether the demand for *Ayurveda* has increased in Kerala due to tourist arrivals.
- Involvement of *Ayurveda* and growth of tourism.
- Opening up of centers outside Kerala for promotion of Ayurvedic tourism.
- The role of promotion of Ayurvedic tourism in creating awareness about its importance globally and among the local population.
- The development of Ayurvedic tourism and its help in further growth of Ayurvedic research and development.

Table 5.9 Principal Components Analysis for the Scores of Scope of Ayurvedic Tourism

Correlations Transformed Variables

	Demand for Ayurveda	*Involvement of Ayurveda in tourism*	*Promotion of overseas*	*Awareness about Ayurveda*	*Growth Ayurvedic research*
Demand for *Ayurveda*	1.000	.445	.317	-.688	-.161
Involvement of *Ayurveda* in tourism	.445	1.000	.077	-.680	.416
Promotion of overseas centers	.317	.077	1.000	-.216	-.551
Awareness about *Ayurveda*	-.688	-.680	-.216	1.000	.076
Growth of Ayurvedic research	-.161	.416	-.551	.076	1.000
Dimension	1	2	3	4	5
Eigen value	2.316	1.672	.551	.340	.121

Source: Field survey at Ayurvedic centers.

The data represented in the above table 5.9 is a result of conversion of multivariable original data into a set of uncorrelated mean, which quantifies and compresses multivariable into a single data. For the factors considered here, we have taken a mean for different variables that are being drawn in x as well as y-axis. Taking an example of the first factor ie, demand for Ayurveda, the author has taken a mean of multivariables like very low, low, average, high and very high as 1.000 for x as well as y axis as the mean of responses for the above mentioned variables. .445 is the result of correlation between the factor, commercialization of Ayurveda with the other factor, involvement of Ayurveda in tourism. This method is followed for all other factors. Here we are considering variables like increase in the demand for Ayurveda due to tourist arrivals, involvement of Ayurveda in the growth of tourism, feasibility of opening up Ayurvedic centers overseas, increasing awareness about Ayurveda globally and locally, growth of Ayurvedic research and development. Correlation analysis helps us in determining the degree of relationship between two or more variables. By using the above statistics, we get the object scores table through various statistical methods like frequencies, modes etc. By using the various variables, we get the following objective scores and objective plots which are shown in Table 5.10.

Table 5.10 Object scores for the variable, scope of Ayurvedic Tourism

Variable Principal Normalization

	Dimension 1	*Dimension* 2
1	.351	.260
2	.263	.983
3	.380	-.360
4	.176	.526

5	.100	.823
6	-1.127	1.021
7	.330	.264
8	-.550	-2.619
9	.781	-1.213
10	.113	.667
11	.493	.424
12	.352	.260
13	-3.966	-.452
14	.129	.202
15	.880	-2.435
16	.364	.104
17	.351	.260
18	.079	.826
19	.401	-.364
20	.100	.823

Source: Field survey at Ayurvedic centers.

The object points in the above table 5.10 are concentrated between 0 and 1. It reveals that Ayurvedic tourism has tremendous scope in Kerala. A graphical representation of the scope of Ayurvedic tourism based on object points received as a result of the study is shown below in Graph 5.7.

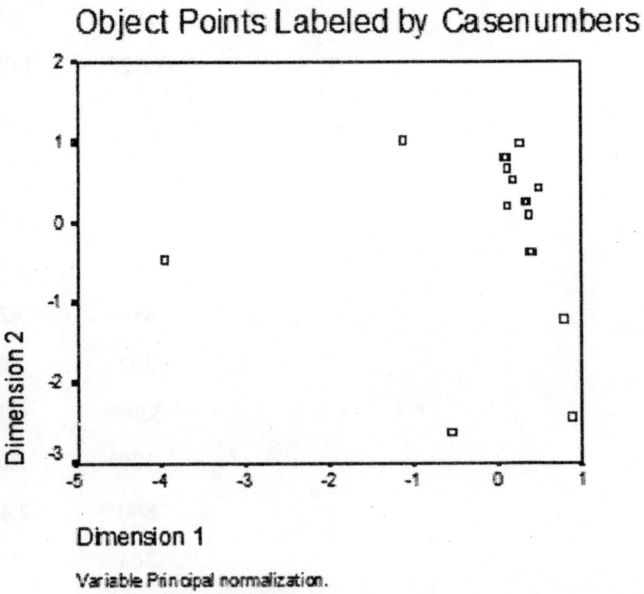

Graph 5.7 Object points labelled by case numbers for the variable, scope of Ayurvedic tourism

Source: Field survey at Ayurvedic centers

In the above graph, the object points are concentrated between 0 and 1. So it is evident that Ayurvedic tourism has tremendous scope in Kerala. Factors like increase in the demand for *Ayurveda* due to tourist arrivals, involvement of *Ayurveda* in the growth of tourism, feasibility of opening up Ayurvedic centers overseas, increasing awareness about *Ayurveda* globally and locally, growth of Ayurvedic research and development were considered for arriving at this conclusion.

Table 5.11

Component Loadings for the scores of Scope of Ayurvedic tourism

	Dimension	
	1	2
Demand for *Ayurveda*	.849	-.099
Involvement of *Ayurveda* in tourism	.750	.533
Promotion of overseas centers	.441	-.713
Awareness about *Ayurveda*	-.910	-.104
Growth of Ayurvedic research	-.104	.927

Variable Principal normalization.

Source: Field survey at Ayurvedic centers.

A plot of the component loadings is displayed in table 5.11. Variables with no multiple nominal scaling levels have component loadings. By component loadings, we are trying to find the significant effect of each variable. For this, we have to calculate component loadings by using different statistical tools. For example, the component loadings for the factor demand for *Ayurveda* is .849 in dimension 1 and -.099 in dimension 2. This method follows for the other factors too. For pictorial representation, we need the two dimensional components which is displayed in the above table. The contribution of various factors analyzed for study, towards the overall performance is shown above. A graphical representation of the contribution of various factors towards the overall performance and the results are shown below in graph 5.8.

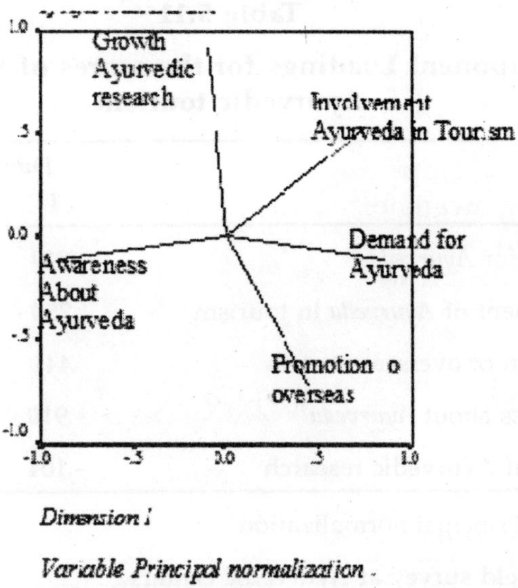

Graph 5.8 Component Loadings for Scores of Scope of Ayurvedic Tourism

For pictorial representation, we need the two dimensional components which is displayed in the above table. The contribution of various factors analysed for study, towards the overall performance is shown above. A graphical representation of the contribution of various factors towards the overall performance and the results are shown below in graph 5.8

From the above graph it is evident that all the factors have significant effect in the variable, scope of Ayurvedic tourism. We can conclude that all factors like increase in the demand for *Ayurveda* due to tourist arrivals, involvement of *Ayurveda* in the growth of tourism, feasibility of opening up Ayurvedic centers overseas, increasing awareness about *Ayurveda* globally and locally, growth in Ayurvedic research and development have a significant effect in the development of Ayurvedic tourism.

From the above graph it is evident that all the factors have significant effect in the variable, scope of Ayurvedic tourism. We can conclude that all factors like increase in the demand for *Ayurveda* due to tourist arrivals, involvement of *Ayurveda* in the growth of tourism, feasibility of opening up Ayurvedic centers overseas, increasing awareness about *Ayurveda* globally and locally, growth in Ayurvedic research and development have a significant effect in the development of Ayurvedic tourism.

Table 5.12

Percentage Analysis for Scores of Tremendous Scope of Ayurvedic Tourism

	Demand for Ayurveda	*Involve-ment of Ayurveda*	*Promotion of overseas centers*	*Awareness about Ayurveda*	*Growth Ayurvedic research*	*Generat-ion of manpower*
			%	%		
Very Low	10.0%	10.0%	10.0%	5.0%	10.0%	10.0%
Low	25.0%	20.0%	30.0%	25.0%	20.0%	15.0%
Average		5.0%	5.0%	15.0%	20.0%	
High	55.0%	55.0%	45.0%	50.0%	45.0%	60.0%
Very High	10.0%	10.0%	10.0%	5.0%	5.0%	15.0%

Source: Field survey at Ayurvedic centers.

Respondents were asked to give their comments on the above factors related to the scope of Ayurvedic tourism. The majority of responses proved that Ayurvedic tourism has tremendous scope in Kerala. A graphical representation of the responses is shown below in Graph 5.9.

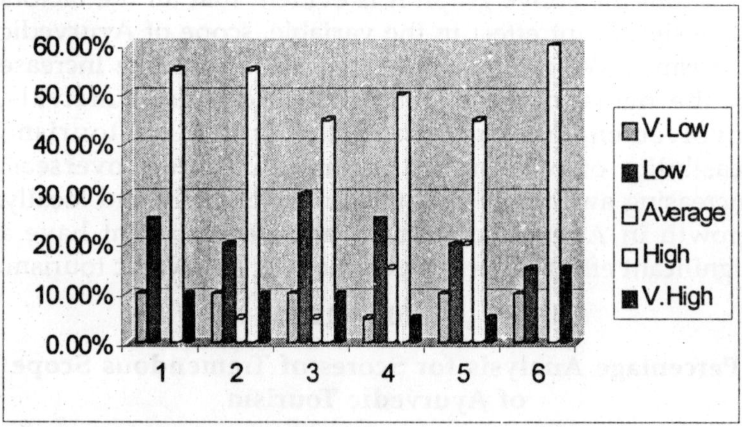

Graph 5.9 Scores of tremendous scope of Ayurvedic tourism.

Source: Field survey at Ayurvedic centers

The above graph proved that Ayurvedic tourism has tremendous scope in the socio economic development of Kerala.

5.6 Principal Components Analysis for the Scores of Socio-economic Development of Kerala

A number of factors related to the socio-economic development of Kerala due to Ayurvedic tourism were analysed. The factors considered for study are the following.

- Whether Ayurvedic tourism development has resulted in the improvement of the status of Ayurveda doctors.
- The need for specific jobs like translators interpreters guides, helpers, masseurs etc.
- Whether Ayurvedic tourism will help in economic growth around treatment centers.
- Whether Ayurvedic treatment at various centers are offered at ayurvedic treatment centers.

Table 5.13

Principal Components Analysis for the Scores of Socio-economic Development of Kerala

Correlations Transformed Variables

	Improvement in status	*Need for specific jobs*	*Economic growth*	*High price*
Improvement in status	1.000	-.520	-.048	-.377
Need for specific jobs	-.520	1.000	.557	.245
Economic growth	-.048	.557	1.000	-.133
High price	-.377	.245	-.133	1.000
Dimension	1	2	3	4
Eigen value	1.895	1.268	.584	.253

Source: Field survey at Ayurvedic centers.

The data represented in the above Table 5.13 is a result of conversion of multivariable original data into a set of uncorrelated mean, which quantifies and compresses multivariable into a single data. For the factors considered here, we have taken a mean for different variables that are being drawn in x as well as y-axis. Taking an example of the first factor ie, improvement of status of Ayurveda doctors, the author has taken a mean of multivariable like very low, low, average, high and very high as 1.000 for x as well as y axis as the mean of responses for the above mentioned variables.

-.520 is the result of correlation between the factors, need for specific jobs. This method is followed for all other factors. Correlation analysis helps us in determining the degree of relationship between two or more variables. The table 5.13 reveals the relationship between factors like improvement in status, need for specific jobs, economic growth and high price.

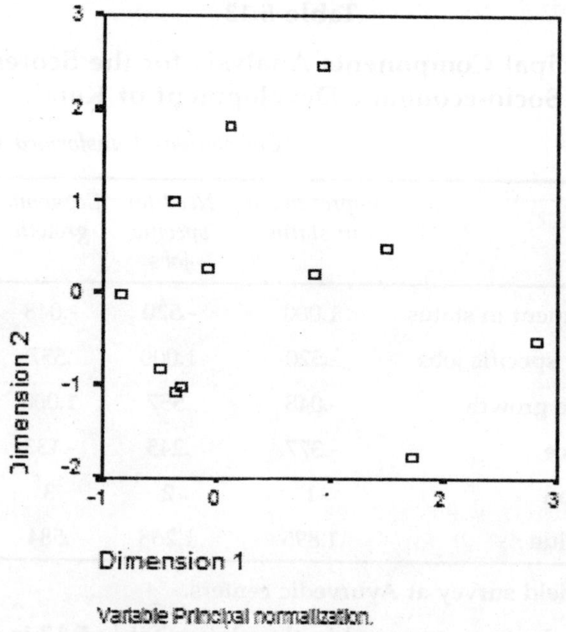

Graph 5.10. Object points labelled by case numbers for Socio-Economic development of Kerala

Here a high variance can be seen in the object points. So the points are scattered. But on observation it is clear that almost all the points are on the positive side. So it concludes that Ayurvedic tourism has significant impact on the socio-economic growth of Kerala. For arriving at this conclusion factors like improvement of the status of Ayurveda doctors, need for specific jobs, economic growth around the treatment centers and the high price charged for treatment were considered.

Table 5.14

Component Loadings for the Scores of Socio-economic Development of Kerala

	Dimension 1	2
Improvement in status	.755	-.375
Need for specific jobs	-.900	-.237
Economic growth	-.528	-.769
High price	-.486	.692

Variable Principal Normalisation

Source: Field survey at Ayurvedic centers.

A plot of the component loadings is displayed in table 5.14. Variables with no multiple nominal scaling levels have component loadings. By component loadings, we are trying to find the significant effect of each variable. For this, we have to calculate component loadings by using different statistical tools. For example, the component loadings for the factor improvement in status are .755 in dimension 1 and -.375 in dimension 2. This method follows for the other factors too. For pictorial representation, we need the two dimensional components which is displayed in the above table. The contribution of various factors analyzed for study towards the overall performance is shown above. A graphical representation of the contribution of various factors towards the overall performance and the results are shown below in Graph 5.11.

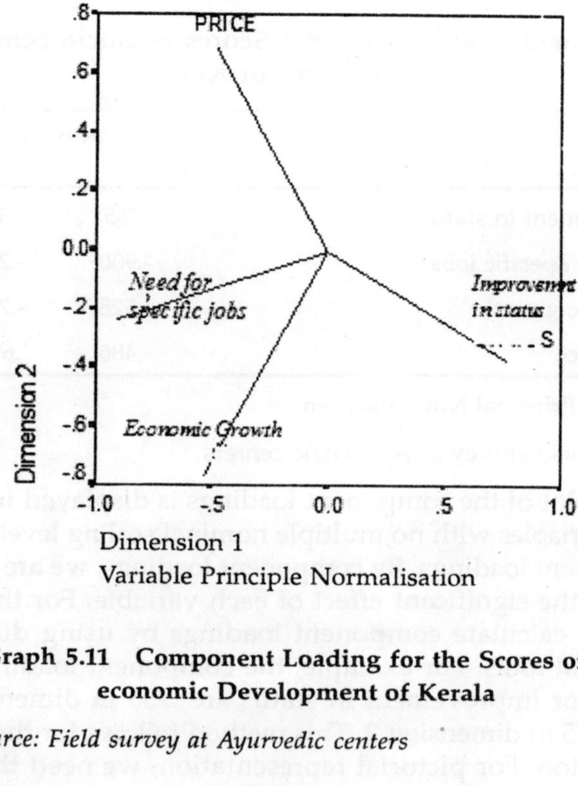

Graph 5.11 Component Loading for the Scores of Socio economic Development of Kerala

Source: Field survey at Ayurvedic centers

From the graph it is evident that all the factors have significant effect in the socio-economic development of Kerala. Factors like improvement of status of *Ayurveda* doctors, need for specific jobs for Ayurvedic tourism industry, economic growth around treatment centers, price charged for Ayurvedic treatments has helped in arriving at this conclusion.

Table 5.15 Percentage Analysis for Scores of Socio-economic development of Kerala

	Improvement in status	*Need for specific jobs*	*Economic growth*	*High price*
Very Low	10.0%	10.0%	5.0%	10.0%
Low	20.0%	20.0%	30.0%	30.0%
Average				5.0%
High	60.0%	70.0%	65.0%	50.0%
Very High	10.0%			5.0%

Source: Field survey at Ayurvedic centers.

Respondents were asked to give their expert views regarding the above factors directly related to socio-economic development of Kerala. These responses proved that Kerala could develop socially and economically through Ayurvedic tourism development. A graphical representation of the responses is shown below in Graph 5.12.

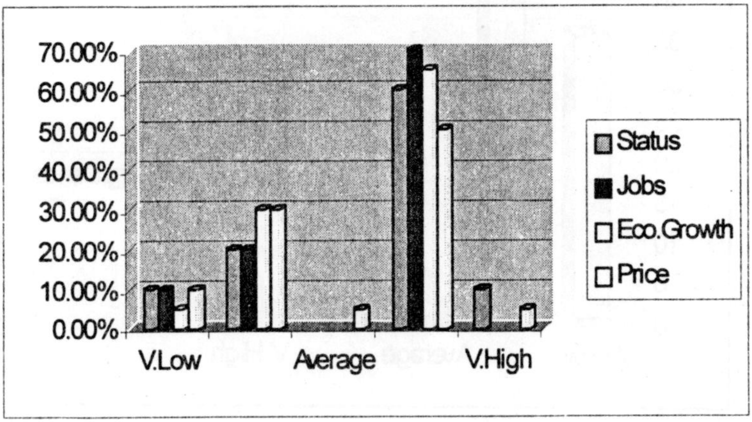

Graph 5.12 Scores of Socio-economic development of Kerala

Source: Field survey at Ayurvedic centers

The above graph shows that Kerala can attain socio-economic development by developing Ayurvedic tourism

Table 5.16

Scores of Right Quality of Medicines and Treatment in Ayurvedic Centers

	Percent	*Valid Percent*	*Cumulative Percent*
Very Low	35.0	35.0	35.0
Low	40.0	40.0	75.0
Average	5.0	5.0	80.0
High	15.0	15.0	95.0
Very High	5.0	5.0	100.0
Total	100.0	100.0	

Source: Field survey at Ayurvedic centers.

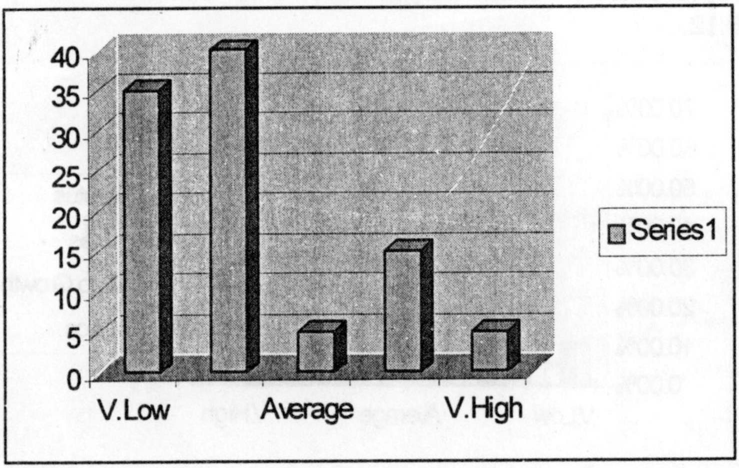

Graph 5.13 Scores of right quality of medicines and treatment in Ayurvedic centers

Source: Field survey at Ayurvedic centers.

The above graph shows that Ayurvedic centers are not offering right quality of medicines and treatment. Presently, there is no mechanism to ensure quality of Ayurvedic medicines. The quality of medicines and the percentage of contents shall be checked and a mechanism for such checking should evolve. For *'Pizhichil'* treatment, minimum seven liters of herbal oil (*thailam*) is required for a seven-day treatment. The price of oil will come to around Rs.3500/-. There are many centers offering treatment at competitive prices, but the quality of medicines is not ensured. There are centers, which are using even perfumed palm oil instead of herbal oil[1]. The famous medicine named *'Dasamoolarishtam'* should contain 71 ingredients including *Kasthuri*. *'Kasthuri'* costs Rs. 25 lakhs per kilogram. For preparing 67.5 litres of *'Dasamoolarishtam'*, 3.75 grams of *'Kasthuri'* is required which will cost more than Rs.10,000[2]. The availability of *'Kasthuri* is also less. Due to all these reasons, most of the drug manufacturers are avoiding addition of certain essential ingredients, which ultimately lessens the quality of the medicines.

Table 5.17

Scores of Adequate Treatment Space and Utensils for Treatment

	Percent	*Valid Percent*	*Cumulative Percent*
Very Low	40.0	40.0	40.0
Low	40.0	40.0	80.0
Average	5.0	5.0	85.0
High	10.0	10.0	95.0
Very High	5.0	5.0	100.0
Total	100.0	100.0	

Source: Field survey at Ayurvedic centers.

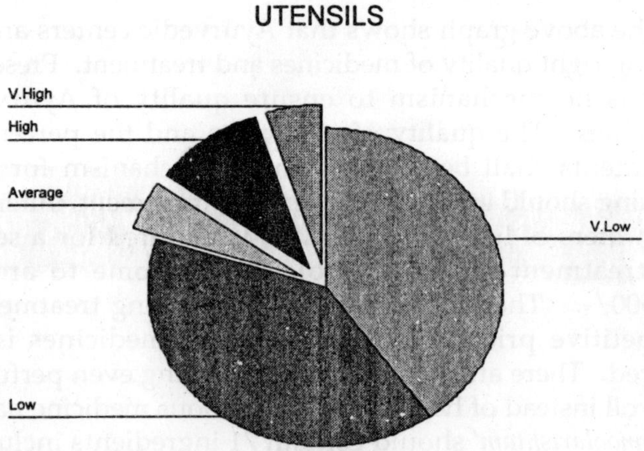

Graph 5.14 - Scores of adequate treatment space and utensils for treatment.

Source: Field survey at Ayurvedic centers.

The above graph shows that most of the Ayurvedic centers are not having adequate treatment space and utensils for treatment. Adequate treatment space, utensils and cleanliness are important for properly discharging Ayurvedic treatments. The government through its classification measures has ensured this in government-approved centers.

Table 5.18 Scores of Presence of Well Qualified Doctors in Ayurvedic Centers

	Percent	*Valid Percent*	*Cumulative Percent*
Very Low	35.0	35.0	35.0
Low	50.0	50.0	85.0
High	10.0	10.0	95.0
Very High	5.0	5.0	100.0
Total	100.0	100.0	

Source: Field survey at Ayurvedic centers.

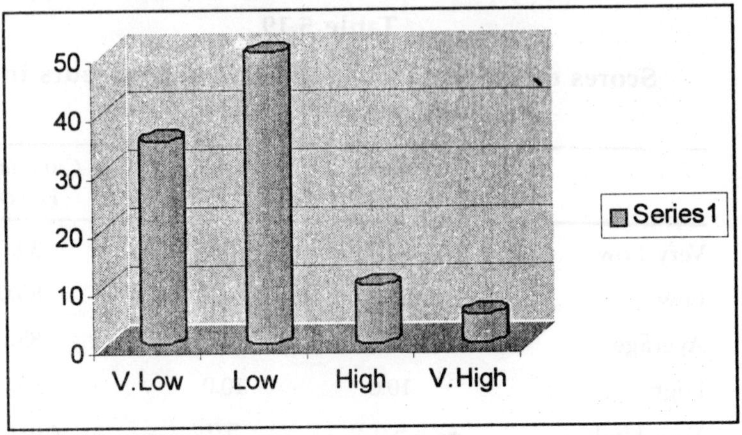

Graph 5.15 Scores of presence of well qualified doctors in Ayurvedic centers

Source: Field survey at Ayurvedic centers

The graph represents the inadequate number of well-qualified doctors in Ayurvedic centers of Kerala. The study revealed that the Ayurvedic centers are not having adequate number of doctors. Many doctors and various departments are managed in big hospitals as well as in certain Ayurvedic resorts. In certain small resorts, there will be a doctor for namesake. Some doctors go to a number of centers for offering treatment. Treatments like *Panchakarma* require proper guidance from a highly trained and skilful Ayurvedic practitioner[3]. This should not be undertaken just from a mere knowledge of *Ayurveda*. One should consult an Ayurvedic physician who is very well qualified. *Panchakarma* is done individually for each person, considering his or her specific constitution and specific disorder. Thus it requires close observation and supervision. But the study proved that most of the Ayurvedic centers around tourist destinations are not having enough well qualified doctors.

Table 5.19

Scores of Presence of Well Trained Masseurs in Ayurvedic Centers

	Percent	*Valid Percent*	*Cumulative Percent*
Very Low	30.0	30.0	30.0
Low	50.0	50.0	80.0
Average	5.0	5.0	85.0
High	10.0	10.0	95.0
Very High	5.0	5.0	100.0
Total	100.0	100.0	

Source: Field survey at Ayurvedic center.

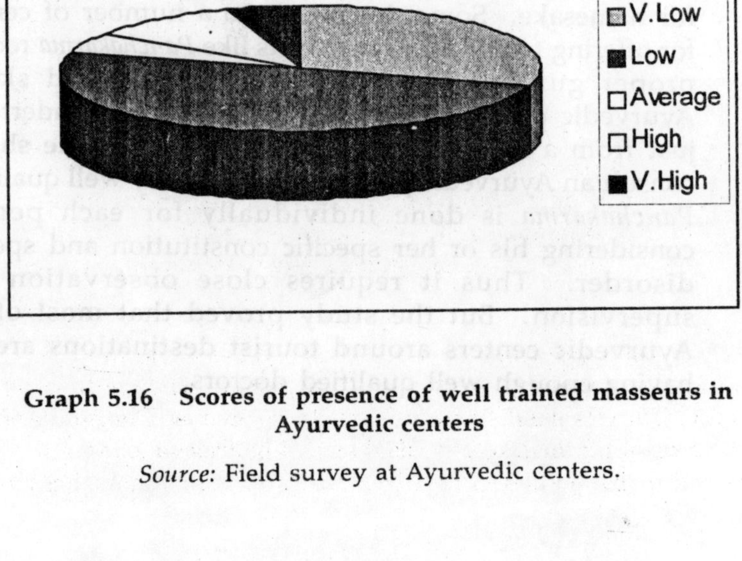

Graph 5.16 Scores of presence of well trained masseurs in Ayurvedic centers

Source: Field survey at Ayurvedic centers.

The above graph reveals that trained masseurs are less in Ayurvedic centers. For offering treatments like *'Kizhi'*, a minimum of four masseurs (technicians) is required. Most of the centers are not having enough number of masseurs. Even the classification scheme brought forward by the department of tourism insists on the presence of only two masseurs. The number of well-trained masseurs who studied the Ayurvedic techniques from well-known institutions is less. The mushrooming of Ayurvedic centers has aggravated this problem.

Table 5.20 Scores regarding traditional Ayurvedic methods in Ayurvedic centers

	Percent	*Valid Percent*	*Cumulative Percent*
Very Low	40.0	40.0	40.0
Low	40.0	40.0	80.0
High	15.0	15.0	95.0
Very High	5.0	5.0	100.0
Total	100.0	100.0	

Source: Field survey at Ayurvedic centers.

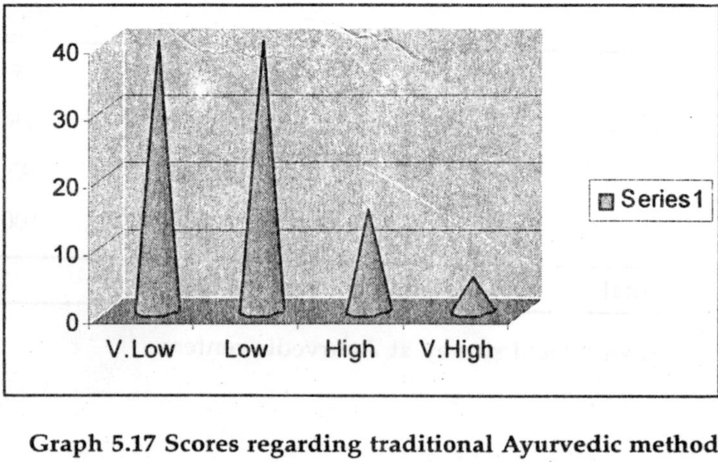

Graph 5.17 Scores regarding traditional Ayurvedic methods in Ayurvedic centers

Source: Field survey at Ayurvedic centers.

The above graph shows that Ayurvedic centers are not following traditional Ayurvedic methods in true spirit. Some resorts offer facility to undergo Ayurvedic treatment of their choice to the tourists. This is against the basics of *Ayurveda*. Improper application of treatments will aggravate the physical condition of patients. All tourists cannot be considered as patients. Proper application of treatments is required even in rejuvenation therapies too. Treatments like *kashayavasti, Snehavasti* etc. cannot be offered individually[4]. But there are centers, which are breaking these rules. The duration of *rasayana* treatment is one month. Most resorts offer this treatment for a duration of seven to fourteen days charging around Rs30,000/-. *Rasayana* treatment requires meticulous preparations and strict diet regimen. The casual approach of certain Ayurvedic centers creates a mistaken notion about Ayurvedic treatments in the mind of the tourists.

Table 5.21

Scores of Duration of Ayurvedic treatment in Ayurvedic Centers

	Percent	*Valid Percent*	*Cumulative Percent*
Very Low	45.0	45.0	45.0
Low	30.0	30.0	75.0
High	20.0	20.0	95.0
Very High	5.0	5.0	100.0
Total	100.0	100.0	

Source: Field survey at Ayurvedic centers.

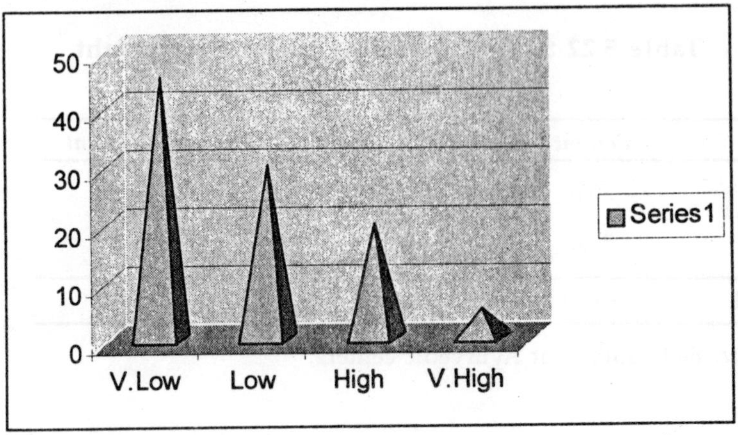

Graph 5.18 Scores of duration of Ayurvedic treatment in Ayurvedic centers

Source: Field survey at Ayurvedic centers

The above graph reveals that the duration of Ayurvedic treatments are not as per Ayurvedic rules. Most of the Ayurvedic centers offer various treatments with the following duration. *Pizhichil* (7 to 21 days) *Njavarakizhi* (14 days) *Takradhara, Ksheeradhara, Thailadhara* (14 days) *Matravasti, Snehavasti, Kashayavasti* (5-25 days), *Shirovasti* (14 days), *Udvarthanam* (14-28 days), *Abhyanga* (14 days), *Snehapanam* (14 days), *Kizhi* (14 days), *Kativasti, Urovasti, Talam,* etc. are offered at various centers. *Rasayana* treatment (14 days), *Kayakalpa* treatment (18 days) etc. are offered to rejuvenate disease-free tourists. For properly offering Panchakarma treatment, 51 days are required. There are centers at Kovalam, which offers Panchakarma in 3 days. The study revealed that most of the centers are not offering Ayurvedic treatments for a proper duration.

Table 5.22 Scores regarding treatment in right season and climate

	Percent	*Valid Percent*	*Cumulative Percent*
No	70.0	70.0	70.0
Yes	30.0	30.0	100.0
Total	100.0	100.0	

Source: Field survey at Ayurvedic centers.

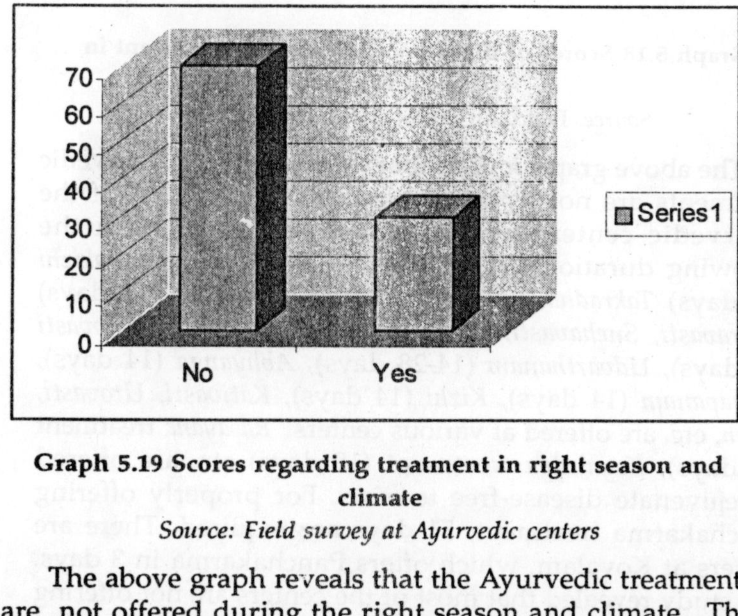

Graph 5.19 Scores regarding treatment in right season and climate

Source: Field survey at Ayurvedic centers

The above graph reveals that the Ayurvedic treatments are not offered during the right season and climate. The monsoon season is the best period for Ayurvedic treatments. Treatment like *Pizhichil* can be offered between 8 A.M to 10.A.M and from 4.P.M to 6.P.M. It requires silent rooms with presence of fresh air. Wind and rain will act as a hindrance. It is difficult to enforce these conditions in Ayurvedic tourist centers. Most of the Ayurvedic centers are not offering treatments during right season and climate.

Table 5.23 Scores of rates quoted for Ayurvedic treatment

	Percent	*Valid Percent*	*Cumulative Percent*
High	70.0	70.0	70.0
Moderate	30.0	30.0	100.0
Total	100.0	100.0	

Source: Field survey at Ayurvedic centers

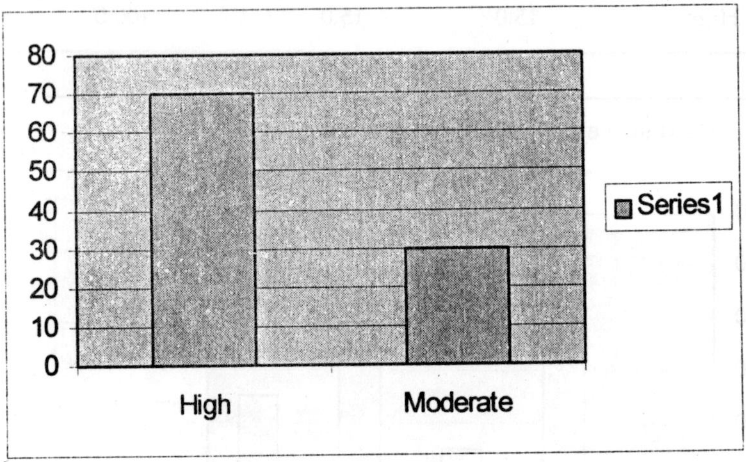

Graph 5.20 Scores of rates quoted for Ayurvedic treatment.
Source: Field survey at Ayurvedic centers.

The above graph revealed that the rates quoted for Ayurvedic treatment in Kerala is high. The study showed that the Ayurvedic centers are quoting widely differing rates for various treatments. Widely differing and high rates are quoted by even well known approved centers.

Table 5.24 Scores regarding commercialization and the quality of medicines

	Percent	*Valid Percent*	*Cumulative Percent*
Very Low	10.0	10.0	10.0
Low	25.0	25.0	35.0
Average	5.0	5.0	40.0
High	45.0	45.0	85.0
Very High	15.0	15.0	100.0
Total	100.0	100.0	

Source: Field survey at Ayurvedic centers.

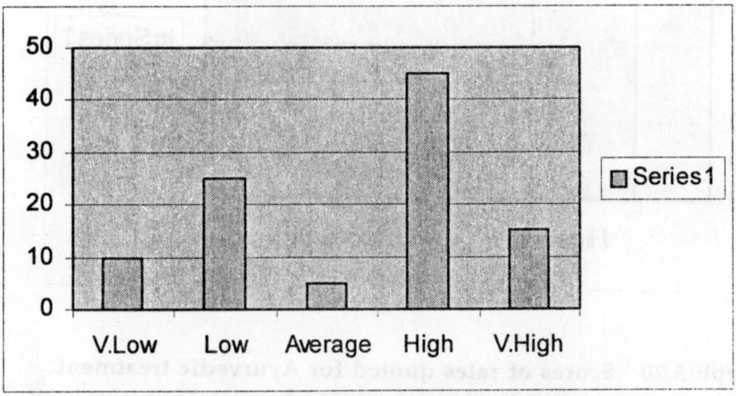

Graph 5.21 Scores regarding commercialization and the quality of medicines

Source: Field survey at Ayurvedic centers.

The above graph showed that commercialization of *Ayurveda* has resulted in lessening the quality of medicines. Commercialization and the huge demand for Ayurvedic products and treatments have resulted in a heavy demand for a number of herbs. Whenever there is a scarcity of a

herb or drug, then the tendency is to replace it by other similar substances. Heavy demand for Ayurvedic products has resulted in the manufacture of medicines in big volumes. Most of the manufactures are not following the exact traditional practices during the manufacture of medicines. For example, *'arishstam'*, an Ayurvedic drug should be kept beneath the earth for a period of one month[5]. But except some drug manufacturers, others are not properly doing the same.

Table 5.25 Scores of Perception of doctor community regarding involvement of tourism in *Ayurveda*

	Percent	*Valid Percent*	*Cumulative Percent*
Very Low	10.0	10.0	10.0
Low	20.0	20.0	30.0
Average	5.0	5.0	35.0
High	55.0	55.0	90.0
Very High	10.0	10.0	100.0
Total	100.0	100.0	

Source: Field survey at Ayurvedic centers.

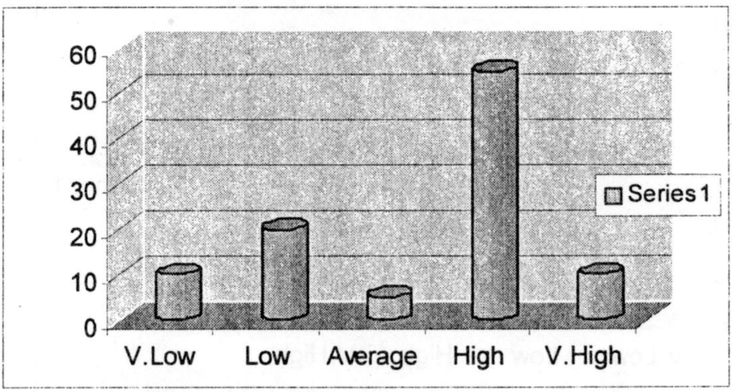

Graph 5.22 Scores of Perception of doctor community regarding involvement of tourism in *Ayurveda*

Source: Field survey at Ayurvedic centers.

The above graph revealed that the involvement of tourism in Ayurveda is congenial to the growth of Ayurveda. Most of the Ayurvedic doctors are considering involvement of tourism in *Ayurveda* as congenial to the growth of *Ayurveda*. Involvement of tourism has created a worldwide interest in *Ayurveda* which will ultimately help it to grow to the level of a global system of medicine. Ayurvedic resorts have also helped in generating good employment opportunities to doctors as well as technicians.

Table 5.26 Scores of Tourist's Willingness to Stay for Adequate Period in Ayurvedic Centers

	Percent	*Valid Percent*	*Cumulative Percent*
Very Low	5.0	5.0	5.0
Low	30.0	30.0	35.0
High	55.0	55.0	90.0
Very High	10.0	10.0	100.0
Total	100.0	100.0	

Source: Field survey at Ayurvedic centers.

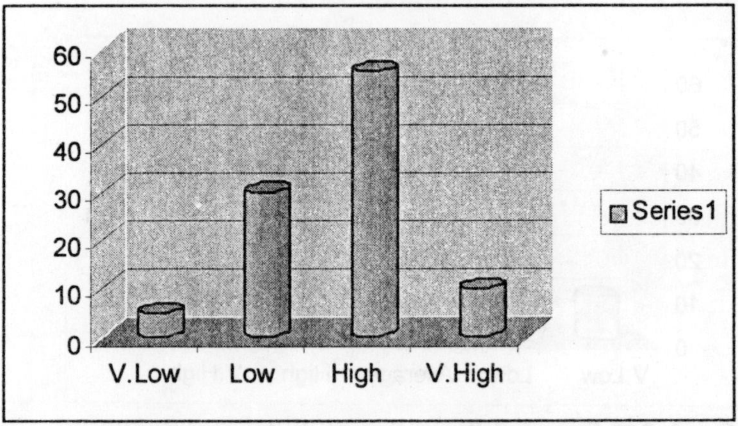

Graph 5.23 Scores of tourist's willingness to stay for adequate period in Ayurvedic centers

Source: Field survey at Ayurvedic centers.

Tourists are willing to stay in treatment centers for an adequate period. Most of the tourists are coming to Ayurvedic resorts after making enquiries about the nature and duration of treatment required for them. As a result, they are staying in these centers for an adequate period. But there is a small section of tourists who are visiting centers due to curiosity and they opt for certain therapies of small duration.

Table 5.27 Scores for difficulties from tourists in discharging treatment

	Percent	*Valid Percent*	*Cumulative Percent*
Very Low	20.0	20.0	20.0
Low	25.0	25.0	45.0
High	50.0	50.0	95.0
Very High	5.0	5.0	100.0
Total	100.0	100.0	

Source: Field survey at Ayurvedic centers.

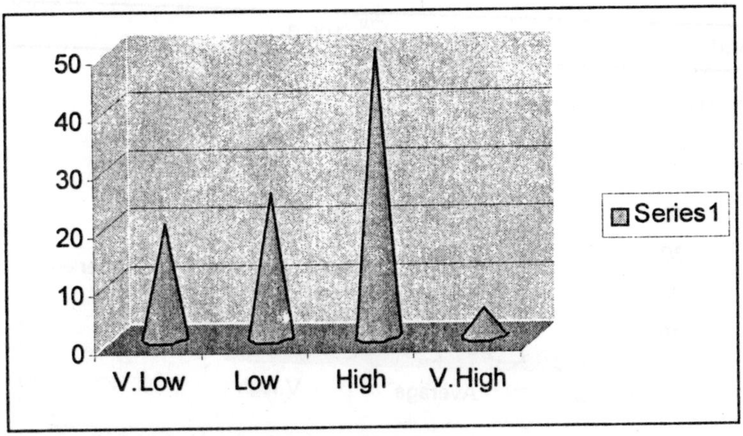

Graph 5.24 Scores for difficulties from tourists in discharging treatment

Source: Field survey at Ayurvedic centers.

The doctor community faces a number of difficulties in properly discharging Ayurvedic treatment. *Ayurveda* is a way of life and diet regimen is one of the important prerequisites for successful treatment. Some of the tourists are not following this properly. The other prerequisites include avoiding loud talk, avoiding journeys, remaining at peace in mind, avoiding exertion, staying away from sleeping during day time and avoiding sexual activity during the treatment days. But most of the tourists, who are coming with an intention of recreation, are not following these basic rules which create difficulties to the doctor community in properly discharging the treatment.

Table 5.28 Scores of bad reputation of Ayurvedic Centers and its effect on tourist arrivals

	Percent	*Valid Percent*	*Cumulative Percent*
Very Low	5.0	5.0	5.0
Low	25.0	25.0	30.0
Average	5.0	5.0	35.0
High	50.0	50.0	85.0
Very High	15.0	15.0	100.0
Total	100.0	100.0	

Source: Field survey at Ayurvedic centers.

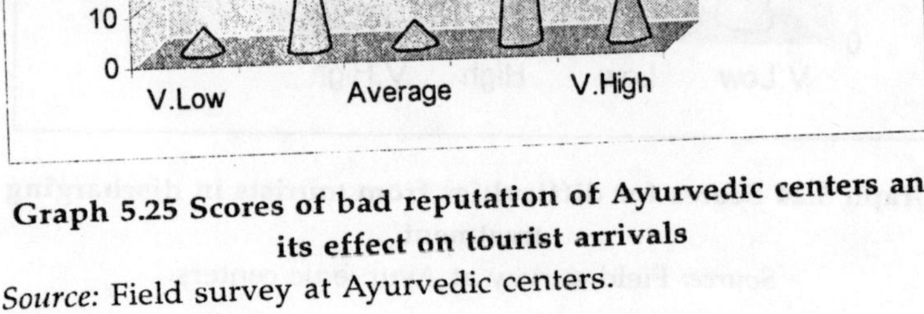

Graph 5.25 Scores of bad reputation of Ayurvedic centers and its effect on tourist arrivals

Source: Field survey at Ayurvedic centers.

The bad reputation of Ayurvedic centers affects tourist arrivals to Kerala. Some of the treatment centers are not following the basic Ayurvedic rules related to quality of medicines, duration of treatment and proper treatment methods. These centers are cheating the tourists. Around thirty centers were forcefully closed down by the government authorities in the year 2000. There are a number of tourists who are approaching these fake centers with bad intentions. These fake centers undermine the good work done by reputed institutions.

Table 5.29 Scores of growth of Ayurvedic tourism and services becoming unavailable to local population

	Percent	*Valid Percent*	*Cumulative Percent*
Very Low	15.0	15.0	15.0
Low	55.0	55.0	70.0
Average	10.0	10.0	80.0
High	20.0	20.0	100.0
Total	100.0	100.0	

Source: Field survey at Ayurvedic centers.

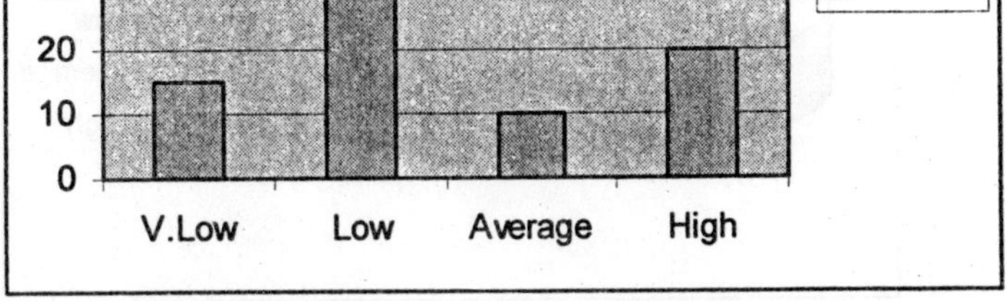

Graph 5.26 Scores of growth of Ayurvedic tourism and services becoming unavailable to local population

Source: Field survey at Ayurvedic centers.

The growth of Ayurvedic tourism has not resulted in the services becoming unavailable to the local population. The interest shown by tourists in Ayurvedic treatment has resulted in the growth of *Ayurveda* as a major medicinal system of Kerala in the last decade. The growth of *Ayurveda* as a medicinal system of global importance has acted as an eye opener to the domestic tourists and local population. The study revealed that increased treatment facilities for tourists have not resulted in the services becoming unavailable to the local community. This shows that these increased facilities are shared by a significant percentage of local population too.

Table 5.30 Scores of Ayurvedic tourism development and fast depletion of herbal wealth of Kerala

	Percent	*Valid Percent*	*Cumulative Percent*
Very Low	15.0	15.0	15.0
Low	50.0	50.0	65.0
Average	10.0	10.0	75.0
High	25.0	25.0	100.0
Total	100.0	100.0	

Source: Field survey at Ayurvedic centers

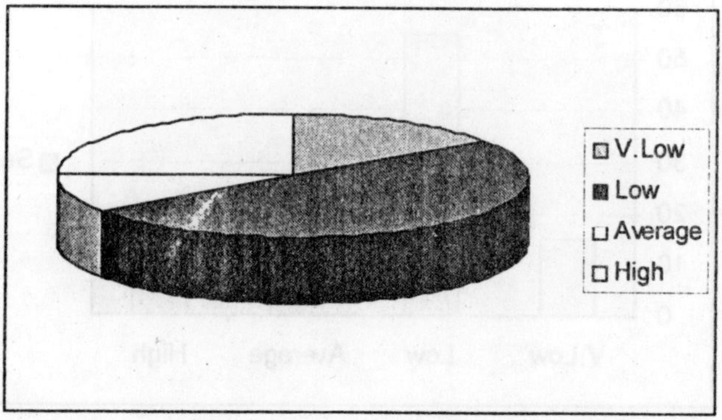

Graph 5.27 Scores of Ayurvedic tourism development and fast depletion of herbal wealth of Kerala.

Source: Field survey at Ayurvedic centers.

Ayurvedic tourism development has not resulted in the fast depletion of herbal wealth of Kerala. The ordinary generic medicines are manufactured using 440 types of herbs. This can be collected from around 380 types of plant species of which 200-250 are available in Kerala[6]. This helps development of *Ayurveda* in Kerala. Use of Ayurvedic herbs in big volumes has opened up new opportunities in the area of its cultivation. Big Ayurvedic companies like *Nagarjuna, Sitaram Pharmacy, Pankajakusturi* etc. are promoting cultivation of herbal plants.

Table 5.31 Scores of fast growth and modernization and its result on deterioration of the quality of medicines

	Percent	*Valid Percent*	*Cumulative Percent*
Very Low	5.0	5.0	5.0
Low	15.0	15.0	20.0
Average	5.0	5.0	25.0
High	60.0	60.0	85.0
Very High	15.0	15.0	100.0
Total	100.0	100.0	

Source: Field survey at Ayurvedic centers

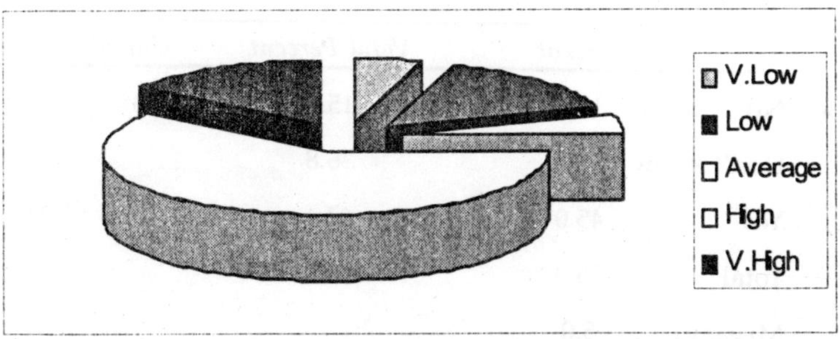

Graph 5.28 Scores of fast growth and modernization and its result on deterioration of the quality of medicines

Source: Field survey at Ayurvedic centers.

It is evident that the fast growth and modernization has resulted in deteriorating the quality of Ayurvedic medicines. Most of the drug manufactures are trying to cope up with the changes which have occurred due to *Ayurveda*'s fast growth and modernization. Manufacture of many medicines requires a complicated process. Medicines like *'arishtam'* should be kept beneath the earth for one month. In the present circumstances, all drug manufacturers are not following exactly the basic principles related to drug production, which ultimately lessens the quality of medicines.

Most of the Ayurvedic medicines like *'Dasmoolarishtam'*; *Punarnavasavam* etc. contain a small percentage of alcohol. During the drug manufacturing process, most of the companies are using *thathiripoo,* a flower which acts as fermenting agent to facilitate fermentation. Some small manufacturers are using chemicals for the process which results in increase in the content of alcohol as well as deterioration in the quality of medicines. *'Dasamoolarishtam'* produced by certain small producers contained up to 28% of alcohol[7]. The study showed that modernization and fast growth of *Ayurveda* has resulted in lessening the quality of medicines.

Table 5.32 Scores of employing female masseurs to lure clients in Ayurvedic centers

	Percent	*Valid Percent*	*Cumulative Percent*
No	15.0	15.8	15.8
Don't know	35.0	36.8	52.6
Yes	45.0	47.4	100.0
Total	95.0	100.0	
Missing	5.0		
	100.0		

Source: Field survey at Ayurvedic centers.

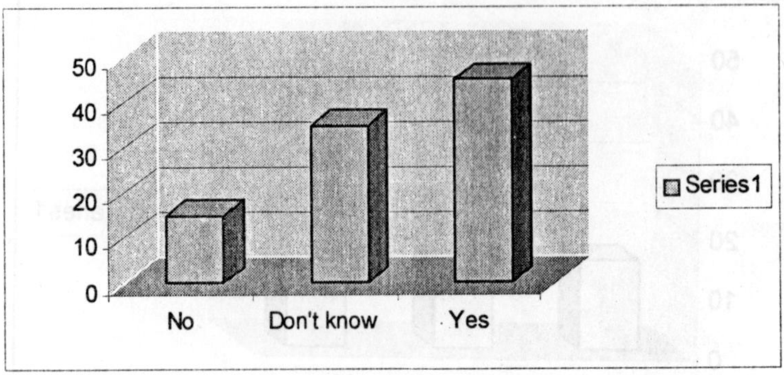

Graph 5.29 Scores of employing female masseurs to lure clients in Ayurvedic centers

Source: Field survey at Ayurvedic centers

The above graph revealed that a significant number of Ayurvedic centers are employing female masseurs to lure male clients. Certain fake centers are engaged in the practice of using female masseurs to lure male clients. Most of these centers are around Kovalam and almost 30 of them were forcefully closed down by the government authorities in the year 2000. The tourists who come without knowing the basics of *Ayurveda* expect sexual favors and massaging promoters of these fake centers.

Table 5.33 Scores of employing male masseurs to lure female clients at Ayurvedic centers

	Percent	*Valid Percent*	*Cumulative Percent*
No	15.0	15.8	15.8
Don't know	35.0	36.8	52.6
Yes	45.0	47.4	100.0
Total	95.0	100.0	
Missing	5.0		
	100.0		

Source: Field survey at Ayurvedic centers.

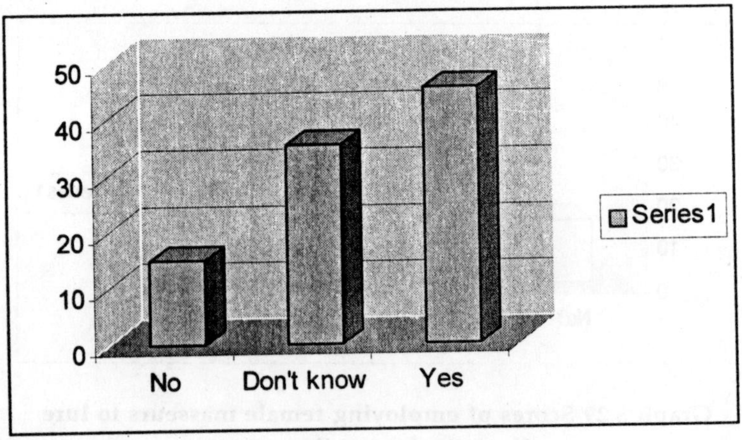

Graph 5.30 Scores of employing male masseurs to lure female clients at Ayurvedic centers

Source: Field survey at Ayurvedic centers

The above graph shows that a significant number of Ayurvedic centers are employing male masseurs to lure female clients. Certain fake centers who are not following the Ayurvedic principles try to exploit tourists by engaging in unethical practices.

Table 5.34 Scores regarding treatments in open air

	Percent	*Valid Percent*	*Cumulative Percent*
No	25.0	27.8	27.8
Don't know	30.0	33.3	61.1
Yes	35.0	38.9	100.0
Total	90.0	100.0	
Missing	10.0		
	100.0		

Source: Field survey at Ayurvedic centers.

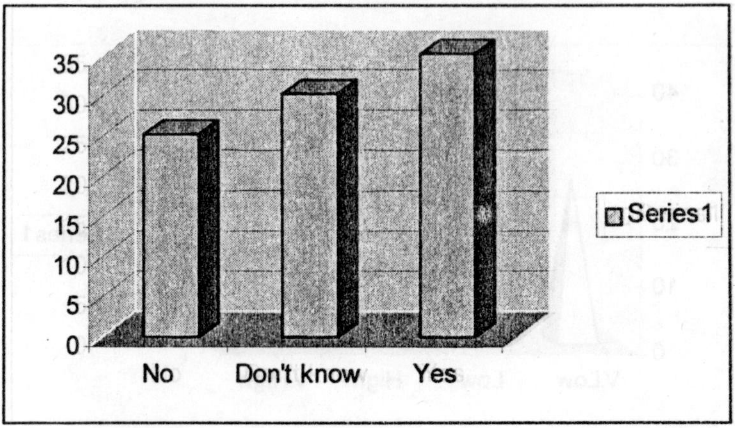

Graph 5.31 Scores regarding treatments in open air.
Source: Field survey at Ayurvedic centers.

It is evident that the massages and treatments are given in open air including beaches by certain Ayurvedic centers. For gaining more tourists, some Ayurvedic centers are using these tactics. This is against the basic principles of *Ayurveda*.

Table 5.35

Scores of clients following diet regimen strictly

	Percent	*Valid Percent*	*Cumulative Percent*
Very Low	25.0	25.0	25.0
Low	30.0	30.0	55.0
High	40.0	40.0	95.0
Very High	5.0	5.0	100.0
Total	100.0	100.0	

Source: Field survey at Ayurvedic centers.

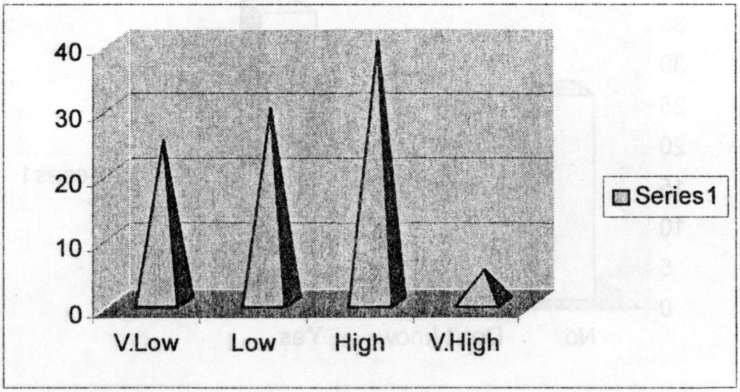

Graph 5.32 Scores of clients following diet regimen strictly
Source: Field survey at Ayurvedic centers

The clients are following the diet regimen strictly during treatment. *Ayurveda* is a way of life and following proper diet regimen is one of its cardinal principles. If the patients are not following strict diet regimen, then the treatment will not give any result. The well known centers are offering suitable diet to the patients depending upon the type of treatment. Treatments like *'Snehapanam'* (consumption of ghee with medicinal properties) demands strict diet regimen for double the number of treatment days. The patient should consume only liquid type of food, which is easily digestible. They should stay away from bad habits like smoking and liquor consumption. Even use of pillow is not permitted. Most of the tourists coming to reputed centers are dedicated tourists willing to explore and follow Ayurvedic treatment methods, which are new to them. But certain centers with good restaurants are not insisting on diet regimen. Some of them even offer boat trips, sight seeing etc. during treatment days which results in exertion to the body. This will not give proper results to the treatment.

Table 5.36 Scores of increase in the demand for *Ayurveda* due to tourism

	Percent	*Valid Percent*	*Cumulative Percent*
Very Low	10.0	10.0	10.0
Low	25.0	25.0	35.0
High	55.0	55.0	90.0
Very High	10.0	10.0	100.0
Total	100.0	100.0	

Source: Field survey at Ayurvedic centers

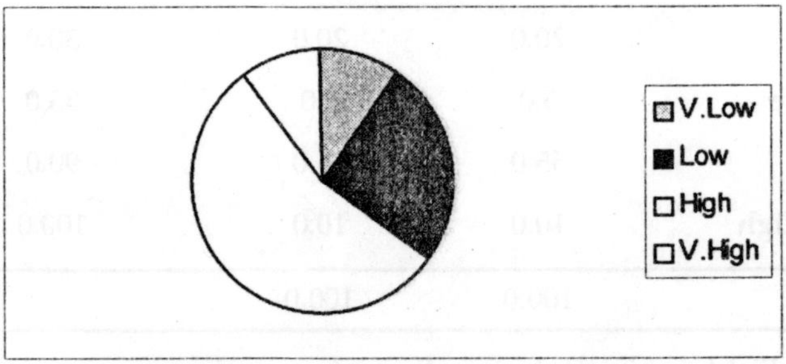

Graph 5.33 Scores of increase in the demand for *Ayurveda* due to tourism

Source: Field survey at Ayurvedic centers.

The demand for *Ayurveda* has increased in Kerala due to tourist arrivals. Global interest in *Ayurveda* has resulted in the mushrooming of Ayurvedic centers in Kerala offering employment opportunities to doctors, technicians, receptionists and a number of people. It had given shape to a category of Ayurvedic centers and spas along with the traditional Ayurvedic hospitals, resulting in the generation of foreign exchange. New employment opportunities to the Ayurvedic doctors are an important result of growth of Ayurvedic tourism. Introduction of

new methods for mass production of medicines and introduction of new machines for offering treatments is another important milestone. Cleanliness and facilities according to western standards is another specialty of Ayurvedic centers. Modernization has helped preparation of traditional Ayurvedic medicines under brand names of which some of them are exported gaining valuable foreign exchange for the country.

Table 5.37 Scores of involvement of *Ayurveda* in the growth of tourism

	Percent	*Valid Percent*	*Cumulative Percent*
Very Low	10.0	10.0	10.0
Low	20.0	20.0	30.0
Average	5.0	5.0	35.0
High	55.0	55.0	90.0
Very High	10.0	10.0	100.0
Total	100.0	100.0	

Source: Field survey at Ayurvedic centers.

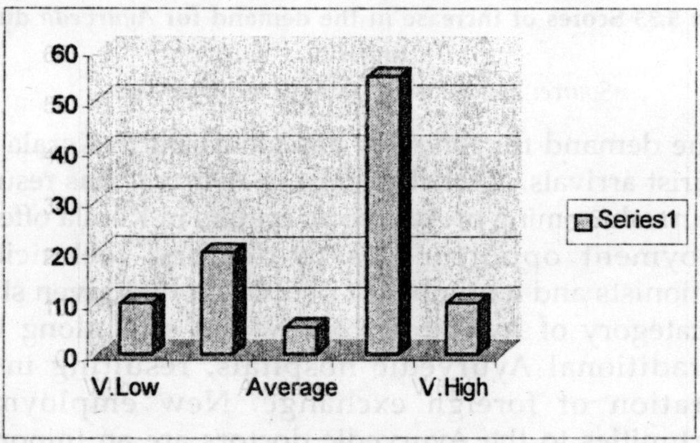

Graph 5.34 Scores of involvement of *Ayurveda* in the growth of tourism

Source: Field survey at Ayurvedic centers.

The involvement of Ayurveda will greatly help the growth of tourism in Kerala. Opening up of Ayurveda to the people of other societies has resulted in creating a global interest on its efficacy. It has helped Kerala in a big way. Foreign exchange earnings from tourism have gone up from the Rs.28.28 crores in 1991 to Rs.535 crores in 2001[8]. Kerala earned foreign exchange worth Rs.1988.40 crores in the year 2006. The total earnings from tourism during 2006 were Rs.9126 crores. The number of foreign tourists has gone up from 50841 in 1986 to 4.28 lakhs in 2006. The number of domestic tourists has increased from 4,23,756 in 1986 to 62.71 lakhs in 2006. The average duration to stay of a foreign tourist in Kerala is 14.1 days[9]. One of the major reasons behind this long duration of stay is the Ayurvedic treatments, which has longer treatment duration. The average annual investment for tourism development in Kerala in 2001 was Rs. 500 crores while the total revenue generated was Rs. 4000 crores[10]. While 1.28 lakh people got direct employment, another 5.18 lakh people got employment indirectly during that year[11]. The average annual investment went up to Rs. 1000 crores in the year 2006. Promotion of Ayurveda as an innovative tourism product will further help growth of tourism in Kerala.

Table 5.38 Scores of putting up overseas centers for promotion of Ayurvedic Tourism

	Percent	*Valid Percent*	*Cumulative Percent*
Very Low	10.0	10.0	10.0
Low	30.0	30.0	40.0
Average	5.0	5.0	45.0
High	45.0	45.0	90.0
Very High	10.0	10.0	100.0
Total	100.0	100.0	

Source: Field survey at Ayurvedic centers.

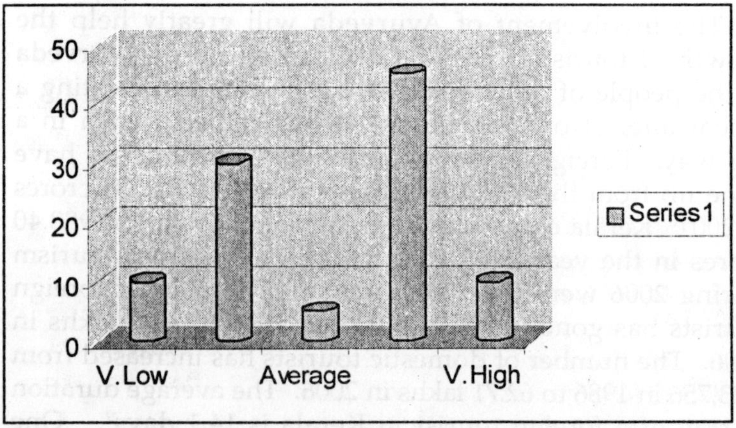

Graph 5.35 Scores of putting up overseas centers for promotion of Ayurvedic tourism

Source: Field survey at Ayurvedic centers.

Ayurvedic centers can be put up outside Kerala for promotion of Ayurvedic tourism. *Ayurveda* is slowly growing as a global medicine. As a result so many foreign countries like Sweden, France, Russia, Germany, Austria, U.K. and U.S.A. are considering it as an alternate system of medicine. The Russian government has recognized Ayurvedic system. Facilities for study, treatment and research have been set up with the technical support of *Aryavaidyasala* of Kottakkal near Calicut. There many problems in practicing *Ayurveda* in foreign countries. While the Western medicine deals with diagnosis, operation techniques and treatment of diseases, Ayurveda deals with prevention of diseases by keeping one healthy. Some of the luxury hotels in Europe are giving certain types of Ayurvedic massages and people misunderstand it as the only thing which *Ayurveda* offers. They do not know the richness and greatness of Ayurvedic treatments.

In western countries, the charges related to medical treatments are borne by insurance companies, which may be a huge amount. Due to negligence of *Ayurveda* by governments, those who undergo Ayurvedic treatments

have to meet the expenses themselves. In Switzerland, insurance coverage is offered to Ayurvedic treatments too while other countries like Germany are not doing the same[12]. Although Ayurvedic treatments are in practice for the last so many centuries, the western world demands scientific confirmation for the various treatments.

Most of the foreign countries are not producing Ayurvedic medicines. They have to procure it from India. As these governments have not given full status of a medical system, Ayurvedic medicines cannot be imported as medicines. For making *Ayurveda* global, attempts should be made to provide genuine medicines or to procure local herbs of same species. In foreign countries no one associated with *Ayurveda* is undergoing the correct clinical training prescribed for degree courses in *Ayurveda*. Lack of deep study of *Ayurveda* and lack of trained hands is an obstacle to Ayurvedic development in other countries. Now the government of Kerala, in its colleges has allotted 10 seats for the students of foreign countries[13]. By slowly solving these problems and by adapting *Ayurveda* to the requirements of western world, *Ayurveda* can be made a global medicine.

Table 5.39 Scores promotion of Ayurvedic tourism and awareness among the local population

	Percent	*Valid Percent*	*Cumulative Percent*
Very Low	5.0	5.0	5.0
Low	25.0	25.0	30.0
Average	15.0	15.0	45.0
High	50.0	50.0	95.0
Very High	5.0	5.0	100.0
Total	100.0	100.0	

Source: Field survey at Ayurvedic centers.

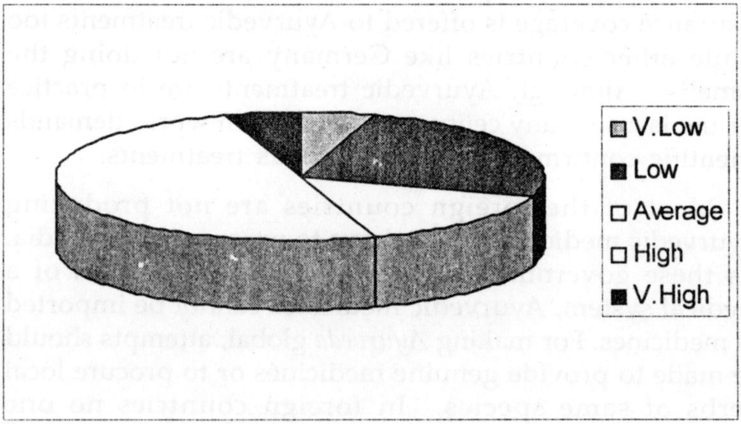

Graph 5.36 Scores of promotion of Ayurvedic tourism and awareness among the local population

Source: Field survey at Ayurvedic centers.

The above graph revealed that the promotion of Ayurvedic tourism will help in creating awareness about its importance globally and among the local population. There are a number of reasons for the growing popularity of *Ayurveda* over the globe. According to Warrier (2002)[14], it is essentially because of people's growing disillusionment with western medicine. "It has failed growing disillusionment with western medicine. "It has failed to deal with chronic problems as well as new, antibiotic-resistant bacteria. *Ayurveda,* by contrast, has an excellent record of curing the sort of chronic problems that do not respond well to the Western medicine. *Ayurveda* can get to the root of the problem". Brennan (2002)[15] says "people in the west are becoming increasingly disgruntled with the detrimental affects of drug therapy. There has been a growing awareness that in modern medicine, the treatments are palliative rather than curative". The globalization of *Ayurveda* is not solely because of the perceived failings of Western medicine. It is also due to the result of shifting social patterns in the west, where the younger generation

in particular is more interested in alternative lifestyles and cultures. Across Britain and Europe, luxury hotels are now offering Ayurvedic packages, which have little more than a massage, some oil treatments and a few herbal products to take home at the end of the weekend along with the complimentary towel and dressing gown. Although these treatments offered there are peripheral in nature when compared to the highly skilled methods of Ayurvedic healing, it has created an interest in *Ayurveda* in those countries. Promotion of Ayurvedic tourism by Kerala has helped in creating awareness about *Ayurveda* globally and also among the local population.

Table 5.40 Scores of growth of Ayurvedic research and development

	Percent	*Valid Percent*	*Cumulative Percent*
Very Low	10.0	10.0	10.0
Low	20.0	20.0	30.0
Average	20.0	20.0	50.0
High	45.0	45.0	95.0
Very High	5.0	5.0	100.0
Total	100.0	100.0	

Source: Field survey at Ayurvedic centers.

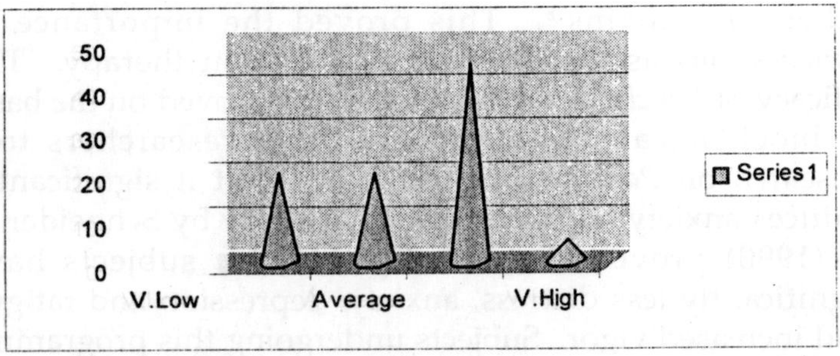

Graph 5.37 Scores of growth of Ayurvedic research and development

Source: Field survey at Ayurvedic centers.

The graph revealed that the development of Ayurvedic tourism will help the further growth of Ayurvedic research and development. *Ayurveda* is very effective in diagnosis and treatment of diseases. Ayurvedic diagnosis is complex and traditionally uses history, pulse and tongue as tools to assess the state and balance of the three major humours in body called *doshas (vata, pitta* and *Kapha)*[16]. Similarly treatment is also individualized and different among patients based on their body constitution. The popularity of *Ayurveda* in the west and its growth as a global medicine demanded scientific clinical evaluation of existing medicines. Proper documentation and registration of medicines and their formulations are required for making *Ayurveda* globally acceptable. The new interest in *Ayurveda* all over the world had showed the importance of further growth of Ayurvedic research and development.

Ayurveda is in practice for many centuries in India. The Western world is demanding scientific confirmation of it for accepting it wholeheartedly. Similar situation occurred with acupuncture too. The acupuncture points were scientifically examined and the differences to the normal skin areas were proved. After this research work, modern medicine accepted acupuncture as a scientific medicine[17]. Similar scientific clinical analysis of Ayurvedic medicines were conducted by various researchers. Scientific analysis of oil samples taken after use in *Panchakarma* therapies in Germany has shown to contain traces of heavy metals and other such toxins[18]. This proved the importance of *Panchakarma* as the foremost purification therapy. The efficacy of *Panchakarma* treatments was proved on the basis of biochemical parameters by other researchers too. Research on *Panchakarma* has found that it significantly reduces anxiety and depression. A study by Schneider et al (1990) proved that the *Panchakarma* subjects have significantly less distress, anxiety, depression and fatigue and increased vigor. Subjects undergoing this programme have shown significantly faster speed of visual processing ability, reduced coronary artery disease risk factors and cardiovascular risk factors[19].

There are a huge number of drug formulations which requires scientific confirmations. Ayurvedic drug formulations are graded according to their smell, taste and colour which are specific to each and every medicine. It means that only an experienced physician or a pharmacist can test these medicines for quality. It is very difficult to test the medicines made with the substitutes, and it is dangerous to test poisonous medicine since it may cause harmful effects to the person who tests the medicine. The subjective experiences of the person testing the medicine are also an important factor. Due to all these reasons, this cannot be taken as an error free method. The development of digital sensors which can smell and taste different materials along with assessing its quality is a gigantic step in the standardization of medicines. This digital sensor technology will help in testing the physical properties of medicines and will provide graphical outputs too. Standardization of Ayurvedic medicines will help it to become a global medicine. The concept of Ayurvedic tourism will further help the growth of Ayurvedic research and development.

Table 5.41

Scores of impact of Ayurvedic tourism on other sectors of economy

	Percent	*Valid Percent*	*Cumulative Percent*
Don't know	5.0	5.0	5.0
Yes	95.0	95.0	100.0
Total	100.0	100.0	

Source: Field survey at Ayurvedic center.

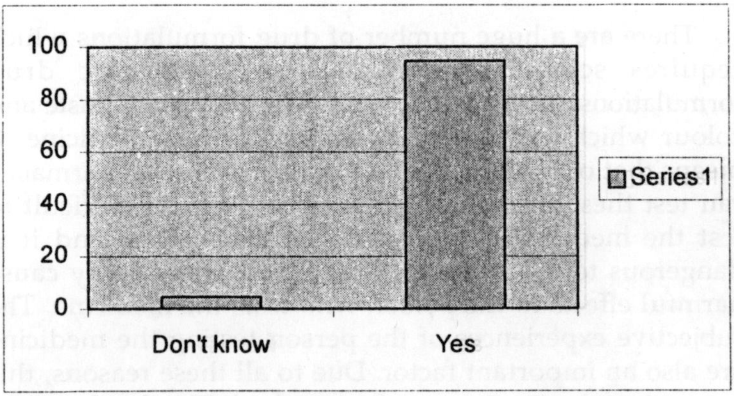

Graph 5.38 Scores of impact of Ayurvedic tourism on other sectors of economy

Source: Field survey at Ayurvedic centers.

The above graph revealed that promotion of Ayurvedic tourism is having a significant impact on other sectors of the economy. The tourist arrivals have a significant economic impact on various sectors of the economy. Tourist receipts are in the form of hotel bills, income from food on trips, beverages, local transport, entertainment, communication, personal care, shopping etc.

Table 5.42

Scores of Ayurvedic tourism and the various sectors of economy

	Hotels	*Transport*	*Handicraft*
No		5.0%	5.0%
Don't No	5.0%	5.0%	5.0%
Yes	95.0%	90.0%	90.0%

Source: Field survey at Ayurvedic centers.

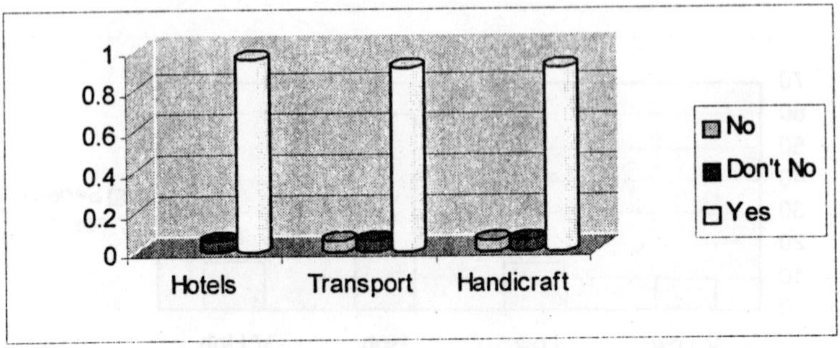

Graph 5.39 Scores of Ayurvedic tourism and the various sectors of economy.

Source: Field survey at Ayurvedic centers.

The above graph revealed that promotion of Ayurvedic tourism is having a significant impact on other sectors like hotels, transport and handicrafts. Abrol of Cox and Kings (2002) says, "Nearly fifteen percent of our bookings are for spas or some kind of Ayurvedic treatment, the sector is booming. This will jump start real estate, hospitality, transport and food and beverage industry. Plus the tourist will spend on shopping[20]." As a result the revenue generated in the Kerala economy due to tourism is assessed as Rs. 4000 crores during the year 2001 which is 6.29% of the gross domestic product of the state. This went up to 9126 crores in 2006.

Table 5.43 Scores of role of Ayurvedic tourism in generation of skilled manpower

	Percent	*Valid Percent*	*Cumulative Percent*
Very Low	10.0	10.0	10.0
Low	15.0	15.0	25.0
High	60.0	60.0	85.0
Very High	15.0	15.0	100.0
Total	100.0	100.0	

Source: Field survey at Ayurvedic centers.

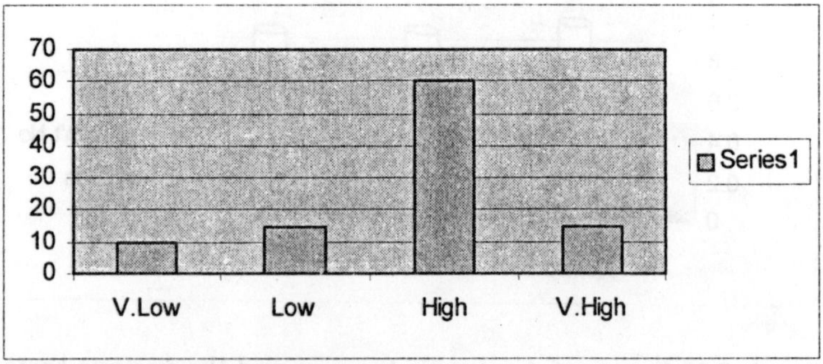

Graph 5.40 Scores of role of Ayurvedic tourism in generation of skilled manpower.

Source: Field survey at Ayurvedic centers.

The graph reveals that promotion of Ayurvedic tourism will help in the generation of skilled manpower required for Ayurvedic treatments. Ayurvedic tourism development has created a multiplier effect on economic growth in different destinations by offering employment opportunities to skilled and non-skilled people in the society. The Ayurvedic centers leads to direct employment generation as each unit has a minimum of one doctor, four masseurs and seven to nine staff members. Some of the Ayurvedic centers have opened overseas centers too resulting in employment opportunities there too.

Table 5.44 Scores of improvement in status of *Ayurveda* doctors

	Percent	*Valid Percent*	*Cumulative Percent*
Very Low	10.0	10.0	10.0
Low	20.0	20.0	30.0
High	60.0	60.0	90.0
Very High	10.0	10.0	100.0
Total	100.0	100.0	

Source: Field survey at Ayurvedic centers.

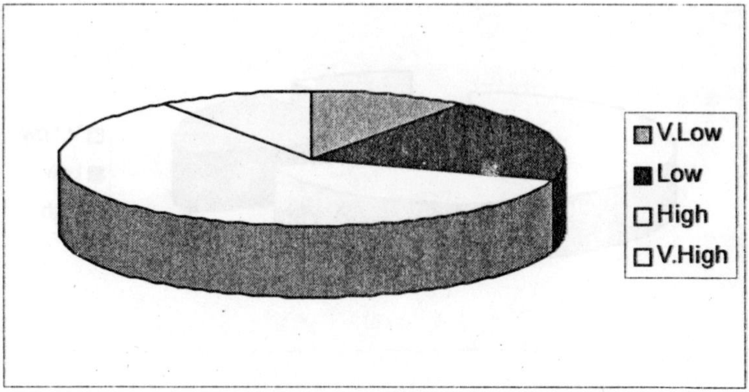

Graph 5.41 Scores of improvement in status of *Ayurveda* doctors

Source: Field survey at Ayurvedic centers

The above graph shows that Ayurvedic tourism development has significantly resulted in the improvement of the status of *Ayurveda* doctors. The status of *Ayurveda* doctors has gone up as a result of the renewed interest in *Ayurveda* all around the world. The income, which the doctors are receiving, has considerably increased. Some Ayurvedic centers of Kerala have opened up Ayurvedic centers abroad which also has resulted in good returns to the doctors employed there. Opening up of a number of Ayurvedic centers has resulted in and creating plenty of job opportunities to the doctors resulting in receiving good returns.

Table 5.45 Scores of need for specific jobs

	Percent	*Valid Percent*	*Cumulative Percent*
Very Low	10.0	10.0	10.0
Low	20.0	20.0	30.0
High	70.0	70.0	100.0
Total	100.0	100.0	

Source: Field survey at Ayurvedic centers.

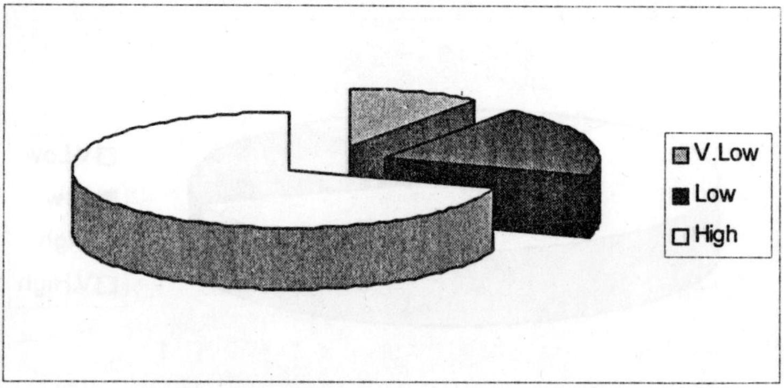

Graph 5.42 Scores of need for specific jobs.
Source: Field survey at Ayurvedic centers.

The graph reveals that there is a great need for jobs like translators, interpreters, guides, helpers and masseurs in connection with Ayurvedic development. Ayurvedic tourism development has produced employment opportunities to handle related jobs. It offered employment opportunities to skilled, semi-skilled and non-skilled people in the society. The direct and indirect employment due to tourism development is estimated at 7 lakhs of which a considerable number is due to resurgence of Ayurveda.

Table 5.46 Scores for economic growth around treatment centers

	Percent	*Valid Percent*	*Cumulative Percent*
Very Low	5.0	5.0	5.0
Low	30.0	30.0	35.0
High	65.0	65.0	100.0
Total	100.0	100.0	

Source: Field survey at Ayurvedic centers.

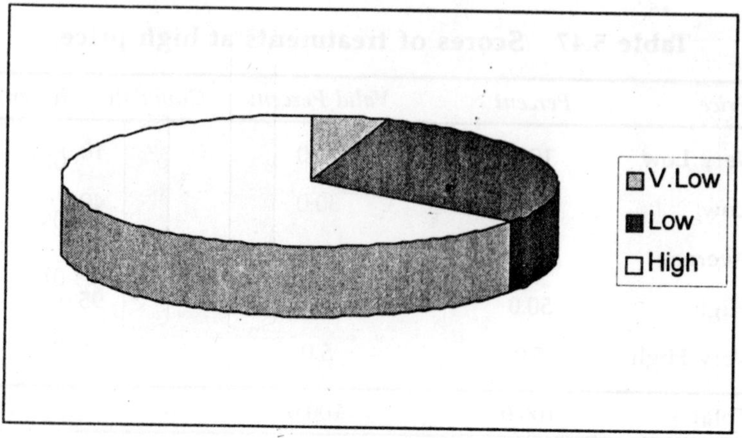

Graph 5.43 Scores for economic growth around treatment centers.

Source: Field survey at Ayurvedic centers.

The graph reveals that Ayurvedic tourism will help in economic growth around treatment centers. Numerous Ayurvedic centers have sprung up in various parts of Kerala in the last decade. It has created employment opportunities to the local population. Tourism is labour-oriented and provides more employment than other industries. Various types of business firms such as hotels, motels, restaurants, tour operators, travel agents, souvenir and gift shops, car rental companies etc. earn a significant percentage of the total spending by the tourists. Several secondary business personnel like construction companies, food and beverage suppliers, photographers, taxi drivers, doctors etc. also benefit out of the tourist spending. Thus growth of tourism can help in economic growth around the treatment centers.

Table 5.47 Scores of treatments at high price

Price	*Percent*	*Valid Percent*	*Cumulative Percent*
Very Low	10.0	10.0	10.0
Low	30.0	30.0	40.0
Average	5.0	5.0	45.0
High	50.0	50.0	95.0
Very High	5.0	5.0	100.0
Total	100.0	100.0	

Source: Field survey at Ayurvedic centers.

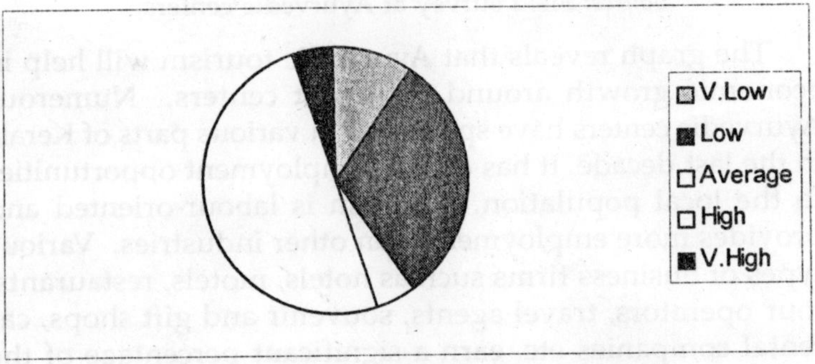

Graph 5.44 Scores of treatments at high price.
Source: Field survey at Ayurvedic centers.

The above graph reveals that Ayurvedic treatments at various centers are offered at high price. Majority of the respondents opined that the Ayurvedic centers are quoting high price for the treatments. Widely differing rates are quoted by the various centers which may confuse the tourists. Most of the centers are quoting the price in terms of dollars. For the high spending tourists, who look for quality treatments, high price is not an issue.

Table 5.48 Scores of enrichment of existing attractions due to Ayurvedic tourism

	Percent	*Valid Percent*	*Cumulative Percent*
No	35.0	35.0	35.0
Don't No	5.0	5.0	40.0
Yes	60.0	60.0	100.0
Total	100.0	100.0	

Source: Field survey at Ayurvedic centers.

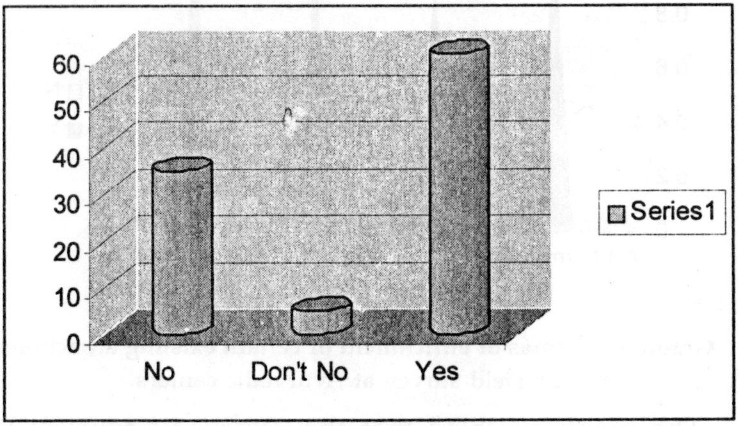

Graph 5.45 Scores of enrichment of existing attractions due to Ayurvedic tourism.

Source: Field survey at Ayurvedic centers.

The above graph reveals that Ayurvedic tourism is enriching the existing tourism attractions of Kerala. Enrichment and diversification of tourism products generally attracts potential tourists. Opening up of *Ayurveda,* the aged medicinal system to tourists has helped Kerala in enriching the existing tourism products and in fast emerging as a major tourist destination. It has also helped in gaining a 100 percent cumulative growth in tourist arrivals in the last five years.

Table 5.49 Scores of enrichment of certain existing attractions

	Art Forms	*Architecture*	*Wild life*	*Crafts*
No		16.7%	8.3%	
Yes	100.0%	83.3%	91.7%	100.0%

Source: Field survey at Ayurvedic centers.

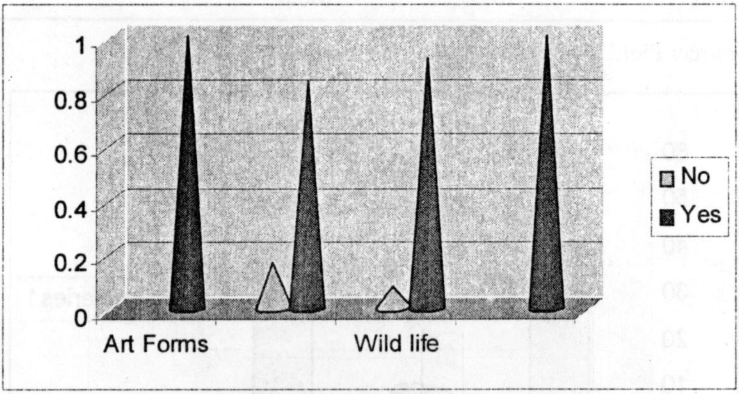

Graph 5.46 Scores of enrichment of certain existing attractions.
Source: Field survey at Ayurvedic centers.

The graph revealed that the Ayurvedic tourism is enriching the existing tourism attractions like art forms and crafts significantly followed by wild life architecture. Kerala is a state with wide range of attractions. They include art forms like *Kathakali, Mohiniyattom* etc. and a number of festivals including the temple festival of *Pooram* held at Trichur. The architectural marvels include temples, palaces etc. The wildlife sanctuaries, crafts etc., also are a part of the Kerala experience. The backwaters of Kerala, a main attraction, are formed by 40 rivers that flow into the Arabian Sea from the Western ghats. Comprising of lakes, rivers, estuaries, the waterways have seen the export of spices to Europe in the past and continue to be a means of transporting goods and people between the interior areas

and the ports. Today these waterways adorn the role of a tourism product with the added attraction of big houseboats. The rich wildlife of Kerala has offered an opportunity to develop eco tourism in a big way in which tourists are heading to explore untouched areas with an educational motive. The introduction of Ayurvedic tourism has enriched the existing wide range of tourism products of Kerala.

Table 5.50 Scores of marketing techniques adopted for promoting Ayurvedic tourism

	Websites	*Word of Mouth*	*Brochures*
Third Pref.	5.3%	10.5%	84.2%
Second Pref.	10.5%	78.9%	10.5%
First Pref.	84.2%	10.5%	5.3%

Source: Field survey at Ayurvedic centers.

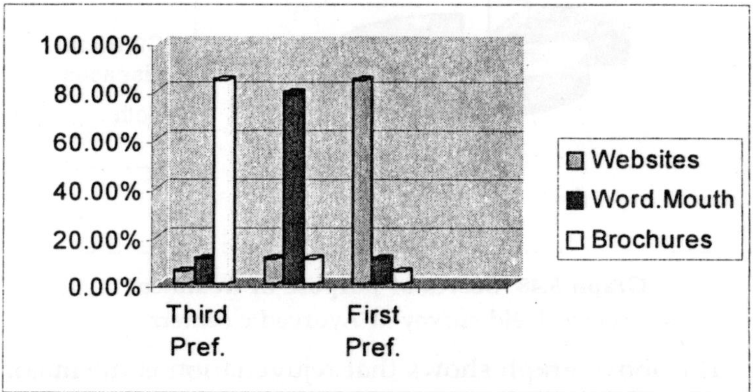

Graph 5.47 Scores of marketing techniques adopted for promoting Ayurvedic tourism.

Source: Field survey at Ayurvedic centers.

The graph reveals that the websites are the preferred marketing tools followed by word of mouth and brochures for attracting Ayurvedic tourists. The majority of the population opined that 84.2%of the international tourists

are attracted to Ayurvedic treatments through websites. The introduction of modern communication means has helped Kerala in gaining much in the form of increased tourist arrivals.

Table 5.51 Scores of purpose of treatment

	%
Rejuvenation	78.9%
Cure from diseases	15.8%
Both	5.3%

Source: Field survey at Ayurvedic centers.

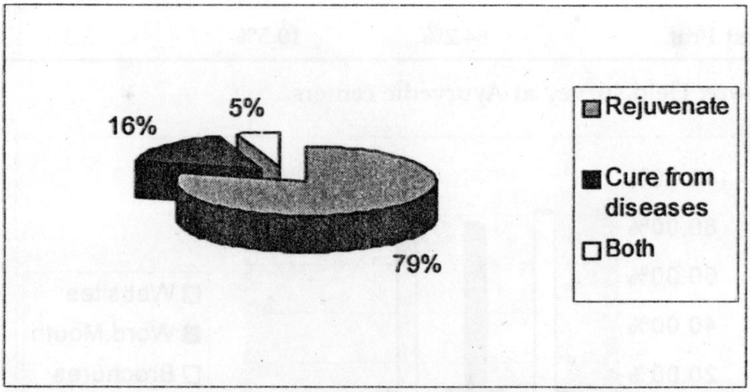

Graph 5.48 Scores of purpose of treatment
Source: Field survey at Ayurvedic centers.

The above graph shows that rejuvenation is the major purpose of Ayurvedic tourist arrivals followed by curative purposes The Ayurvedic procedures, followed in Kerala are meant for curing diseases like insomnia, rheumatism, joint pains, paralysis, hemiplegia, arthritis, nervous disorders, headaches etc and also for eradicating diseased conditions. Some treatments are exclusively meant for the purpose of rejuvenation. The study revealed that 78.9%

of the tourists are visiting Ayurvedic centers for the purpose of rejuvenation while 15.8% are for cure from diseases.

Table 5.52 Scores of repeated visits by tourists

	%
No	10.5%
Yes	89.5%

Source: Field survey at Ayurvedic centers.

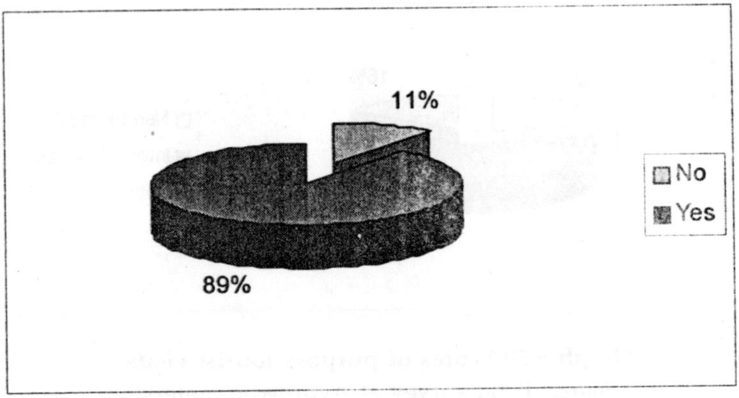

Graph 5.49 Scores of repeated visits by tourists.
Source: Field survey at Ayurvedic centers.

The graph showed that a great number of repeated visits are occurring for Ayurvedic treatments to Kerala. The study revealed that 89.5% of the tourists are interested in visiting the Ayurvedic centers again. This shows the efficacy of Ayurvedic treatments and the better results, which resulted in rejuvenating the body and curing the diseases. Repeated visits will help in gaining more income. It is having a direct impact on increased future tourist arrivals by the publicity created through word of mouth. There were 10.5% of respondents who expressed their intention of not visiting Kerala again for Ayurvedic treatments.

Table 5.53 Scores of purpose tourist visits

	%
Need Based	15.8%
Interest Based	63.2%
Both	21.1%

Source: Field survey at Ayurvedic centers.

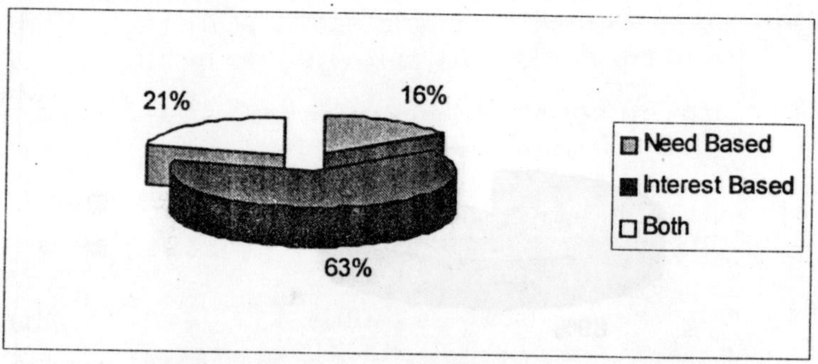

Graph 5.50 Scores of purpose tourist visits.
Source: Field survey at Ayurvedic centers.

The graph reveals that the purpose of tourist visits to Ayurvedic centers are mainly interest based. The study proved the reason behind tourist visits. Majority of the tourists are visiting Ayurvedic centers due to their interest in the Vedic medical science. The curiosity to experience the miracles of *Ayurveda* is the basic reason behind the tourist arrivals. A significant percentage (21.1%) of tourists has opted for Ayurvedic treatments not only due to curiosity and interest, but also due to certain medical needs. The needs can be cure from diseases. The percentage of such need based tourists is 15.8%.

Table 5.54 Salary analysis of Ayurveda doctors

Salary	*Percentage*
3000-5000	30%
5000-7000	20%
7000-9000	15%
9000-11000	15%
Above 11000	20%

Source: Field survey at Ayurvedic centers.

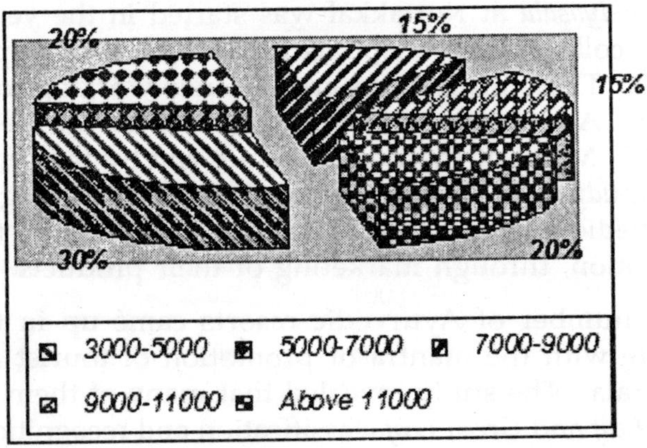

Graph 5.51 Salary analyses of Ayurveda doctors.
Source: Field survey at Ayurvedic centers.

The study revealed that there is a substantial increase in the income of Ayurveda doctors due to the introduction of Ayurvedic centers for tourists. The status of Ayurveda doctors have gone up as a result of Ayurvedic tourism development. While 30% of doctors are receiving an income ranging from Rs. 3000.00 to Rs. 5000.00 another 20% of doctors are receiving Rs. 5000.00 to Rs. 7000.00. Another 15% are in the category of Rs. 7000.00 to Rs.9000.00 and Rs.9000.00 to Rs. 11000.00 each. A significant finding is that

a considerable 20% doctors are receiving more than Rs. 11000.00 monthly as income or salary.

5.7 Ayurvedic Institutions in Kerala

The study showed that Ayurvedic treatments are offered in three categories of organizations. They are

- *Ayurveda* colleges and Hospitals
- *Ayurveda* resorts
- Hotels

Ayurveda colleges and hospitals are in the field of Ayurvedic healthcare for the last so many years. The *Aryavaidyasala* at Kottakkal was started in the year 1902. These colleges and hospitals made Ayurveda popular in Kerala. These institutions are sincerely working to ensure quality Ayurvedic treatment facilities to the people of Kerala. Many of these colleges are run by the renowned *"ashtavaidyas"* of Kerala. Although they are offering quality Ayurvedic treatments, they are not in the field of tourism promotion, through marketing of their products.

A number of Ayurvedic resorts came up in the last decade with the mantra of promotion of tourist arrivals to Kerala. The study revealed that many of them got the *Olive Leaf* and *Green Leaf* classification and recognition from the department of tourism, Kerala and is offering quality treatment to the tourists. These resorts are offering dedicated Ayurvedic treatments led by qualified doctors and technicians where the duration of treatment ranges from one day to as many as 51 days. The number of tourists to these centers is less. But the duration of the treatments are high since, these centers are offering complete and exclusive Ayurvedic treatments. These resorts made the concept of Ayurvedic tourism popular in Kerala.

In Kerala, most of the hotels are also offering Ayurvedic treatment facilities. But the duration of treatments are short.

Although most of the hotels offer only treatments of shorter durations, they attract more tourists when compared to Ayurvedic resorts. Ayurvedic spas have become an essential part of the hotels of Kerala. Along with these institutions, a number of shady parlours are also offering Ayurvedic treatments flouting the basics of *Ayurveda* therapy. Although traditional Ayurvedic hospitals, Ayurvedic resorts and hotels are offering Ayurvedic treatments, more treatment centers with good facilities are required as the number of tourists is increasing. The need of the hour is Ayurvedic centers with excellent standards. More centers assuring cleanliness and quality of treatments are required for increase in future tourist arrivals.

5.8 Resorts and Spas

Resort-based development is one of the most common forms of modern tourism. A tourist resort can be defined as a destination area that is relatively self-contained. It typically provides a wide range of tourist facilities and services including those designed for recreation and relaxation. Holiday villages are also a type of resort. Some resorts are very large with a variety of types of accommodation including self- catering units and many recreation and commercial facilities[21]. Some resorts may be composed of only one hotel and offers a range of facilities, services and activities. Resort hotels differ from traditional hotels in different ways. They offer relaxation and are located in areas that take advantage of attractive natural features. The first resorts in America and Europe were built around spas and focused on health and escape from the daily rigors of life. Although the purpose of resorts is to provide rest, relaxation and rejuvenation, later they began to expand by crossing to other market segment too[22].

The word *spa* means "a *mineral spring*", but the use of this term has been expanded in recent years to describe a place where people go to rejuvenate bodies and minds.

Although the various spas may differ in their operating focus, the basic ingredients of the spas include healthy food, exercise classes, baths, massages, herbal treatments and educational training programs[23]. Spas employ massage therapists who can perform different types of massages and other body treatments. The general spas employ cosmetologists and aestheticians who can perform make up. Fitness employees conducts fitness classes and co-ordinate certain recreational activities. Spas employ spa assistant or attendants who can supervise the locker rooms, maintain cleanliness and perform some body treatments. It offers employment opportunities to front office people who can meet and greet guests and schedule all guest service[24]. For achieving total customer satisfaction, well trained staff is required.

5.9 Economic Impacts

Tourism is a powerful force for economic and social development creating employment and wealth. Money, time and physical energy to travel is required for successful travel. Small amount of these resources will decrease the ability to travel while a large amount of these resources will increase the tourist's ability to travel. Rich western people like to travel to developing nations like India, which are attractive for a variety of tourism resources including health therapies.

Many countries and states like Kerala, have determined that development of their tourism resources can add to the economic well-being of the area. Many countries believe that tourism has a comparative advantage over other industries on economic, social and environmental fronts. Tourism may have comparative advantage over other industries in the following ways. The destination may be specially appealing to tourists because

- It has features that are highly attractive.
- It may be accessible to many potential tourists.

- It has the necessary infrastructure and an abundant labour force to serve in the tourism industry[25].

Kerala has all these ingredients which will result in huge tourist arrivals. It is well known for a wide range of attractions like backwaters, eco tourism, houseboats, martial arts, rich wildlife, art and art forms etc. Ayurvedic therapy is a unique attraction of the state. The state is accessible due to the presence of three airports with international services. The rich human resource acts as a boost for the state's tourism industry. Tourism may also be the best industry for so many states if there are no alternatives. For small states like Kerala, there are fewer alternatives for economic development. Tourism provides a wide variety of job opportunities at various levels.

- Entry level employment for relatively unskilled and semiskilled workers.
- Employment for highly skilled craft persons.
- Professional level opportunities for well-educated decision makers

Ayurvedic tourism in Kerala created a number of attractive employment opportunities to doctors, masseurs, technicians; receptionists' etc. Tourism often provides improved infrastructure facilities that can be enjoyed by residents as well as tourists. Opening up of more Ayurvedic centers brought more facilities which can be shared by the local residents too. It brought about an interest in the age-old medicinal system locally and internationally resulting in new studies on various aspects.

In states like Kerala, receipts from tourism may provide an infrastructure which in turn forms the base for the diversification of the economy and for the development of other industries. Tourism expenditure can stimulate economy beyond the areas concerned with tourism. Tourism creates a multiplier effect in the economy after the visitors spend money on a wide variety of goods and services. This money is injected into the society in various

forms which ultimately benefits the local community. Mostly in tourism industry, a significant part of the earnings will be spent for importing goods meant for tourists. As a result the benefit will leak away from the local community. Since *Ayurveda* is indigenous and uses traditional resources, practices and facilities, the earnings remain in the economy boosting it. The achievements in the form of income, new jobs and amenities for the resident population can be regarded as the major beneficial effects of tourism in a tourist destination.

5.10 Social Impacts

Tourism can create positive and negative impacts on the society. Any influx of tourism will make some impact on the area as the host community shares different value systems. The development of the tourism product will be determined by the type of tourism activity as well as the socio-economic characteristics of the tourists. The social and economic impact of tourism on the host population is partly determined by the tourism product[26]. The impact brought about by the interaction of hosts and tourists has been exemplified in a model devised by Valene Smith. According to her, explorers or tourists whose main interest is to meet and understand people from different cultures will fully accept and acclimatize to the foreign culture. Ayurvedic centers in Kerala mainly receive such tourists who are keen on understanding the Indian system of medicine and practices. They understand the richness and uniqueness of Indian way of life and adapts fully with the circumstances. This reduces the scope for host-tourist encounters.

There is a significant positive socio-cultural impact which includes the preservation of ancient monuments, historic building and sites, traditional arts, crafts and customs. In Kerala, most of the age old houses constructed on Kerala style *(Nalukettu* and *Ettukettu)* were refurnished to start Ayurvedic centers. Most of these damaged splendid

big houses were dismantled and carefully reconstructed at tourist destinations.

Some view tourism as a bridge between people, fostering communication, mutual understanding and a desirable redistribution of wealth. If tourism development is not managed properly and economic benefits are no realized, it will create resentment to tourism activity. Some view tourism as a cause of envy and enmity due to the difference in wealth between tourists and hosts. Tourism sometimes acts as a threat to traditional values, customs, beliefs and identity of host culture. Increased cost of living, congestion, greater pollution and crime can create social tension too. High crime rates, gambling, drinking and prostitution are also some ill-effects of tourism development. All these create irritation among hosts. Doxey drew up an index to measure the level of irritation generated by guest-host contacts[27].

- *The level of euphoria:* The initial enthusiasm that comes along with the launch of tourism activities. At this stage the tourists are made welcome and the number of visitors is few.
- *The level of apathy:* In this growth stage, the number of visitors accelerates rapidly. The hosts consider tourists as a source of profit making and the interaction is on a formal basis.
- *The level of irritation:* In this stage of maturity, the number of visitors continues to increase at a slower rate. Here as the industry approaches saturation point, the hosts' shows irritation as they can no longer cope with the number of tourists without additional facilities.
- *The level of antagonism:* At this point of saturation, tourists are considered as unwanted and hosts turn antagonistic towards them.

In the final stage of decline, the number of tourist arrivals will come down. The level of social impact can be determined by a number of factors including the capacity constraints of the destination. A graphical representation of the impact of guest-host interaction in the product life cycle stage is shown in graph 5.52.

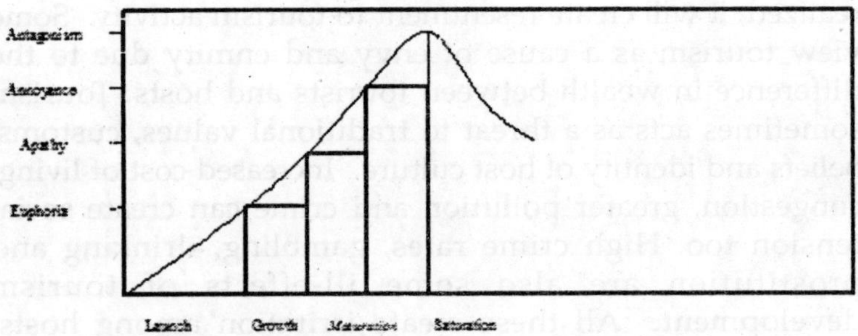

Source : Compiled by Author

Graph 5.52: Impact of guest-host interaction in the product life-cycle stage devised by Doxey.

Kerala with a huge density of population shall opt for explorers and high income tourists who are ready to acclimatize with the local culture, tradition and ways of life.

5.11 The Role of Marketing

In tourism, marketing assumes significance as it is concerned with the assessment of consumer demand. Philip Kotler defines "marketing as a social and managerial process by which individuals and groups obtain what they need and want through creating and exchanging products and value with others[28]. Krippendorf has defined marketing in tourism as follows "Marketing in tourism is to be understood as the systematic and the coordinated execution of business policy by tourist undertakings whether private or state owned at local, regional, national

or international level to achieve the optimal satisfaction of the needs of identifiable consumer groups and in doing so to achieve an appropriate return."[29]

The tourism industry is spending huge sums of money on developing new attractions, improving products and for building the infrastructure. The way in which the risk level can be minimized only through the adoption of a marketing strategy which provides products related to the needs of consumers.

5.11.1 The Service Product

Tourism and hospitality products come under service products and have specific characteristics which are different from other products. The intangible nature of tourism products means that the product cannot be easily evaluated or exhibited before its purchase. The benefits of tourism products can be demonstrated through printed literature and other audio visual means only. The inseparable nature of tourism product focuses on interpersonal relationships where the performance level of the staff is directly related to the satisfaction and experience of the consumer. Variability or lack of consistency in the performance of a product is another nature of service products. Service products cannot be stored for sale on a later occasion as they are perishable in nature. If Ayurvedic centers are left empty it means that revenue can be never recouped. The characteristics of service products are applicable to Ayurvedic holidays too. The potential tourists are not in a position to evaluate the quality of services offered at Ayurvedic centers. The treatment requires experienced doctors and skilled masseurs as the treatments cannot be separated from the personnel who are offering it. The success of Ayurvedic holidays will largely depend on the demonstration of realities in the publicity material. It should be an unbiased depiction of the realities as the customers will go for a thorough property analysis keeping in mind the following factors.

- Variety of services
- Appeal of services
- Consistency
- Pricing
- Service speed
- Service Quality
- Facilities
- Atmosphere
- Brand image
- Promotional activity
- Service friendliness
- Cleanliness

If the expectation of the tourists is not to the expected level, the product will fail in the market. Gronroos (1982) has developed a model to explain what he calls as the 'missing service quality concept'[30]. He tried to explain the gap between the expected service and perceived service. It distinguishes between 'technical quality' and 'functional quality'. Technical quality refers to what the customer is actually receiving from the service. Functional quality refers to how the technical elements are offered. The tourist in an Ayurvedic center will evaluate not only the quality of the age-old Ayurvedic treatments, but also the way in which it is offered. It includes the style, manner and appearance of the staff working there.

5.11.2 Marketing Orientation

The tourism industry requires a marketing orientation which deals with careful formulation of the products[31]. They should engage in marketing research to identify the customers changing needs. The purpose of majority of the tourists opting for Ayurvedic holidays is rejuvenation

while some are looking for cure from diseases. It means that the target market shall be identified to analyze the marketing opportunities. Translating the needs of the customers by careful product planning and formulation is the next step. A careful pricing policy reflecting the product's value at different seasons is another important aspect. Then the product shall be made available to the market. Informing and motivating the customer for purchase through promotion is another important function. These tasks and marketing functions are applicable to Ayurvedic centers too who are offering health packages.

There are several methods used in the conduct of a marketing campaign which includes advertising, development of a sales force and the use of public relations. The effectiveness of the advertising campaign depends mainly upon the credibility of the message conveyed by the advertisement through the visual and print media and the extent of coverage achieved by the campaign. Tourist literatures in the form of brochures, prospectuses, folders etc. are other mediums of marketing in tourism. Modern communication mediums like websites are widely used by Ayurvedic centers. The study revealed that 84.2% of the foreign tourists to Kerala coming for Ayurvedic treatments are attracted by websites, followed by word of mouth and brochures. Product oriented marketing approach highlighting the unique features of products like *Ayurveda* can help development of tourism in Kerala.

5.12 Ayurvedic Tourism and Associated Problems

The results of the research showed that there is a significant scope in *Ayurveda* for the development of tourism in Kerala. The involvement of Ayurvedic treatment in tourism and its demand on international tourism markets have made some of the practitioners to think in terms of business. Such matters transformed into the psyche of tourism business personnel, the result was the mushrooming of Ayurvedic centers in different developed tourist

destinations. "People were interested in it and so we pursued it. We did not anticipate this unprecedented growth in the number of Ayurvedic centers" (T. Balakrishnan)[32]. However due to business mentality, the service providers could not identify the future dangers of unprecedented growth of Ayurvedic tourism and ignored it right from the initial stages of development.

The population opined almost unanimously that there is a significant increase in the number of Ayurvedic centers without having adequate quality of facilities and services. "Though a few resorts are providing genuine treatment, the majority of them are interested in making money (P.S. Syamalakumari)[33]. It may be noted however that, the traditional system of treatment realized the problem of fading reputation. Many of the Ayurvedic centers in Kerala are using medicines of lower quality and engaged in unethical practices. Some Ayurvedic centers are not having adequate treatment space and necessary utensils. The only exceptions are the reputed hospitals and the centers approved by the department of tourism, Kerala. The government authorities are yet to control these highly unethical acts. There is no mechanism for monitoring the quality of herbal medicines. "If the manufacturing company is registered, the products do not require separate license" (Venkitakrishnan)[34]. In the case of Ayurvedic medicines, the manufactures are asked to register with the Drugs controller and acquire Good Manufacturing Practice (GMP) certification which is a mark of standardized procedures to ensure cleanliness and appropriate ingredients. Many of the herbal products have managed to evade such restrictions.

Climatic conditions also have a significant impact on treatment results. Ayurvedic treatment can give excellent results in monsoon season, when the atmosphere is cool and the body is receptive to oils and therapy. The ultimate aim of projecting *Ayurveda* as a tourism product was to ensure Ayurvedic tourism activity during monsoon, which

is generally not a tourist season. But from the initial stages itself, the market has taken control over the principles of *Ayurveda* regarding treatment seasons. Most of the tourists are coming to Kerala during the tourist season between October and March to receive Ayurvedic treatments which is exactly not the best season for Ayurvedic treatments.

In Kerala, availability of some herbs is limited. But the demand for such herbs like *"Kottam"* is very high. The supply and resource availability does not meet at equal ratio. This is due to the adulteration or substitution of the original herbs. Unavailability and depletion of herbal resources will offer a new opportunity in the area of its cultivation.

Most of the Ayurvedic centers located near to the Kovalam beach have flouted basic norms of Ayurvedic treatment. There are some shady parlours which employ female masseurs to lure clientele. Massages and treatment being given in open air on the beach. Diet regimen is not being strictly followed. Patients are deceived, as some of the centers use substandard medicinal products. Widely differing rates are charged for treatments.

During the months of June and July, when tourist arrivals are low the operators offer heavy discounts which results in cut throat competition. During that period, tariffs are low. This opportunity can be used to attract the middle income domestic tourists.

Some other factors like length of stay, food habits, and willingness to act according to Ayurvedic rules affect the results of the Ayurvedic treatment. Most of the tourists coming to Kerala want to cover maximum places in minimum number of days. They may not practice the preconditions for effective Ayurvedic treatment. Rules which have to be strictly followed during treatment are flouted and this will have detrimental effects on the health of the patients.

A bad reputation about Ayurvedic treatment centers is growing along with Ayurvedic development. Such a feeling has developed in the minds of tourists, which may ultimately hamper the growth of such centers. The high tariff has made a hallow effect on its vicinity and may spread all over the industry gradually. The result will be the unavailability of Ayurvedic services to the local people.

5.13 Scope of Ayurveda

There is an experimental proof that thirty percent of tourist arrivals are for health holidays. The statistics shows that Ayurvedic treatments have paved the way for the growth of tourism in Kerala. The promotion of *Ayurveda* on the banner of tourism and vice versa received a global support. As a result the export of Ayurvedic products from India to other countries increased from Rs.145 crores of 1999-2000 to Rs.220 crores in 2000-2001. The global herbal market is expected to grow to Rs. 2,50,000 crores by the year 2010[35]. The European Union has relaxed its norms of 15-year usage criteria under the Herbal Medicinal Product Directive that posed technical barriers to the Indian exporters of herbal products. With this relaxation of its rules, any manufacturing unit can file a dossier of their products having less than fifteen years of documented usage in any of the European Union countries and such a product can be considered for market authorization. This will help India; especially Kerala with its traditional base to grab a large chunk of the European market.

The Ayurvedic tourism development created a multiplier effect on economic growth in different destinations. The employment opportunities increased from highly skilled to non-skilled people in the society. The public in general looks at the destinations as a viable source of income. The Ayurvedic centers leads to employment generation as each unit has a minimum of one doctor, four masseurs and seven to nine staff members.

The global attention towards *Ayurveda* created awareness to the requirement of skilled manpower for the industry. The establishment of various *Ayurveda* colleges in different parts of Kerala will help to ensure quality supply of manpower. The global attention towards *Ayurveda* resulted in the convening of world *Ayurveda* Congress at Cochin during November 2002.

Tourism development coupled with Ayurvedic tourism development helped the society as its beneficiaries. The main benefits which Kerala has received are in the form of increased communication with other people, improved self image of Kerala society in other countries, growing variety of employment opportunities, educational opportunities, motivation for learning, modernization of infrastructure and increased urbanization.

The international tourists are mainly attracted to Ayurvedic treatments through websites. The faulty illustration of details in certain websites has confused the tourists. The trend of marketing also has changed along with the consumer demand. As marketing tools, websites are followed by information through word of mouth and brochures. The study revealed that 90% of the customers in approved *Ayurveda* centers are from foreign countries.

The research also proved that the majority of tourists visited Ayurvedic tourist centers for rejuvenative purposes. The reason is being the increased health consciousness of foreigners and lack of fear on side effects. The repeated visits of customers to approved *Ayurveda* centers shows the quality and efficacy of treatments offered there.

From the above study it could be found that *Ayurveda*, the system of indigenous medicine is in a critical growth stage. Haphazard development and unethical practices will result in the unnatural death of this new emerging trend in tourism development. Introduction of *Ayurveda* as a tourist product has resulted in the vertical growth of income in the last decade. Opening up of this indigenous system

of medicine cautiously and properly will result in the all round socio-economic development of Kerala.

References

1. Divakaran, R.V.M. (2001); *Ayurvedam Vinodamakumbol*, Mathrubhumi Arogyamasika (Malayalam), Kozikode, p. 105.
2. Biju, C.P. (2001); *Paramparryathinte Putiyamugham*, Mathrubhumi Arogyamasika (Malayalam), Kozikode, p. 113.
3. Lad, Vasant (2001); *An Introduction to Panchakarma*, Science India, Thiruvananthapuram, p. 46.
4. Divakaran, R.V.M. (2001); *Ayurvedam Vinodamakumbol*, Mathrubhumi Arogyamasika (Malayalam), Kozikode, p. 105.
5. Biju, C.P (2001); *Paramparryathinte Putiyamugham*, Mathrubhumi Arogyamasika (Malayalam), Kozikode, p. 113.
6. *Ibid.*, p. 114.
7. Bindhu, Quality Controller, Nagarjuna Herbal Concentrates Ltd, Thodupuzha, Kerala, Interview on 05-11-02.
8. Tourist Statistics (2000); Department of Tourism, Thiruvananthapuram, Kerala, p. 26.
9. *Ibid.*, p. 43.
10. *Spreading the Spirit of Tourism*, Brochure, Department of Tourism, Thiruvananthapuram, Kerala, p. 2.
11. Tourist Statistics (2000); Department of Tourism, Thiruvananthapuram, Kerala, p. 43.
12. Namboothiri, Krishnan, Chief Physician, Nagarjuna Ayurvedic Center, Kaladi, Kerala, Interview on 01-11-02.
13. Nair, Krishnan C.K. (2002); *Ayurveda and Western World*, Souvenir, World *Ayurveda* Congress, Kochi, P-26.
14. Stock, Jon, (2002); *Ayurveda* goes Global, *The Week*, Kottayam, p. 16, July 28.

15. *Ibid.*, p. 17.
16. Vinjamury, Sivarama, Singh, Betsy & Mishra, Lakshmi (2002); Compendium of invited Lectures, World *Ayurveda* Congress, Kochi, p. 188.
17. Mathew, Sebastian (2002); *Compendium of invited Lectures,* World *Ayurveda* Congress, Kochi, p. 244.
18. Pohlmann, Adiram, Michaela, Alaxandru (2002); *Compendium of invited Lectures,* World *Ayurveda* Congress, Kochi, p. 9.
19. Mahadevan, l. (2002); *Compendium of Invited Lectures,* World *Ayurveda* Congress, Kochi, p. 83.
20. *Returning to roots,* (2002); *The Week,* Kottayam, July 28.
21. World Tourism Organisation (1995); National and Regional Tourism Planning Routledge, New York, p. 17.
22. Cook, Roy A., Yale, Laura, Marqua, Joseph (1999), *Tourism—the Business of Travel,* Prentice Hall, New Jersey, p. 171.
23. *Ibid.*, p. 179.
24. Monteson, Patricia A. & Singer, Judith (1992, June); *Turn Your spa into a winner,* The Cornell Hotel and Restaurant Administration Quarterly, p. 42.
25. Cook, Roy A., Yale, Laura, Marqua, Joseph (1999); *Tourism-The Business of Travel,* Prentice Hall, New Jersey, p. 224.
26. Cooper, Chris, Fletcher, John, Gilbert, David, Wanhill, Stephen (1993); *Tourism Principles and Practice,* Pitman, London, p. 98.
27. *Ibid.*, p. 102.
28. Kotler, Philip (1996); *Marketing for Hospitality and Tourism,* Prentice Hall, New Jersey, p. 18.
29. Ghosh, Bishwanath (2000); *Tourism & Travel Management,* Vikas Publishing, New Delhi, p. 158.
30. Cooper, Chris, Fletcher, John, Gilbert, David, Wanhill, Stephen (1993); *Tourism Principles and Practice,* Pitman, London, p. 233.

31. *Ibid.*, p. 236.
32. *An Ideal Getaway* (2002); *The Hindu* (Coimbatore), January 27.
33. *Packaging health and a holiday* (2002); *The Hindu* (Coimbatore), January 20.
34. *Nutrients being touted as medicines* (2002); *The Hindu*, (Coimbatore), August 9.
35. *The masseur's reach* (2002); *The Week* (Kottayam), July 28.

6

Health Tourism and Ayurveda in a Nutshell

6.1 Introduction

The development of tourism will have a significant impact on the economies of various countries. Tourism development based on Kerala's available resources will help in solving its wide range of economic problems. Tourism has an impact on economic, social, cultural, political and environmental fronts. These impacts can be positive or negative and the government should consider the costs and benefits before opting for an all round tourism development involving a number of tourism products.

This research was intended to analyze the various issues involved in the field of Ayurvedic tourism development in Kerala. It revealed that inadequate quality of services and facilities are major obstacles in the Ayurvedic tourism development of Kerala. It also highlighted the tremendous scope of Ayurvedic tourism in Kerala's socio-economic development.

The study proved that some Ayurvedic centers are not offering medicines and treatments of right quality to tourists. The quality of medicines and its right usage in right proportion is required for getting maximum benefit out of the treatments. By purely following the traditional treatment methods given in the classical texts, quality of treatments can be ensured.

All Ayurvedic centers in Kerala are not having adequate treatment space and utensils. Except the reputed hospitals like *Aryavaidasala* of *Kottakkal*, hospitals run by some of the *'Ashtavaidyas'* and centers approved by the tourism department, other centers are mostly not having the various utensils and adequate treatment space required for treatments. There are number of fake centers running with various names like Ayurvedic beach resort, Ayurvedic health resort, Massage and rejuvenation center etc. at tourist destinations like Kovalam, Varkala, Palakkad, Alappuzha etc. Most of these centers are not having the adequate treatment space and the number of utensils required for offering proper treatment.

The study proved that majority of Ayurvedic centers is not having well qualified doctors. Complicated treatments like Panchakarma can be offered only under the guidance of experienced doctors. Absence of well-trained masseurs and technicians do more harm than good. Even the Ayurvedic colleges are not running enough training programmes to train masseurs. In some Ayurvedic centers, treatments are selected by the customers, which is against the basic rules of Ayurveda. Customer shall be offered treatments according to the requirement only. Treatments, which cannot be offered independently, are offered in certain centers.

Most of the Ayurvedic centers are not following strictly the rules related to duration of treatments which may prove harmful. Sometimes such treatments may not give any result at all. Ayurvedic treatment will give excellent results in monsoon season when the atmosphere is cool and the

body is receptive to oils and therapy. By projecting *Ayurveda* as a tourism product, the aim was to ensure Ayurvedic tourist arrivals during monsoon, which is not a tourist season. But that experiment failed and majority of the tourists are coming during the tourist season between October and March for receiving treatments. Domestic tourist can be attracted to Ayurvedic centers during the monsoon months by giving discounts too. Treatments shall be offered during right season, climate and time to receive maximum result. Widely differing and high rates are charged by most of the treatment centers. Moderate rates can sustain the trend for a long time as well as can attract more tourist arrivals.

Commercialization and demand for Ayurvedic products in huge volumes has resulted in lessening the quality of medicines. Most of the drug manufactures are not in a position to follow exactly the traditional manufacturing practices during the manufacture of medicines due to heavy demand. Majority of the *Ayurveda* doctors are considering involvement of tourism in *Ayurveda* as beneficial to its growth. It will help it to grow to the level of a global system of medicine. Most of the tourists in Ayurvedic centers are coming exclusively for that purpose and are ready to stay for adequate period. Following strict diet regimen is one of the preconditions for succe sful treatments. Avoiding physical exertion is the most difficult thing for tourists. Some of the tourists are not ready to follow the strict Ayurvedic rules which cause difficulties to the doctor community.

Development of Ayurvedic centers for the foreign tourists has been shared by the domestic tourists too. This is a classic example of how tourism development and related facilities are helping the local population too. The facilities added for tourism development always helps the local population. The ordinary generic medicines can be manufactured from around 380 types of plant species of which 200-250 are available in Kerala. This helps

development of *Ayurveda*. During certain seasons, the supplies of certain herbs are less. During that period, supply of herbs and resource availability does not meet at equal ratio. This is due to the adulteration or substitution of the original herbs which may affect the quality of medicines. Unavailability and demand for herbal resources will create new opportunities in the area of its cultivation.

Many Ayurvedic centers located in Kovalam beach has flouted the basic rules of *Ayurveda*. Some fake parlours are even employing female masseurs to lure clientele. The tourists who are coming without knowing the basics of *Ayurveda* expecting sexual favours are the promoters of these fake centers. Some Ayurvedic centers are offering treatments in open air, especially beaches which is against the basics of *Ayurveda*

New employment opportunities to doctors, technicians, masseurs, receptionists etc. are one of the important facts of Ayurvedic tourism development. The status of Ayurveda doctors have gone up as a result of Ayurvedic tourism development. The study revealed that the employees are receiving increased salary income due to increased Ayurvedic tourist arrivals. Cleanliness and superior facilities according to western standards is another specialty. Modernization and increased interest in *Ayurveda* has helped in the preparation of traditional Ayurvedic medicines under brand names. Many of those medicines are exported after scientific clinical analysis earning valuable foreign exchange. The growth of *Ayurveda* as a global medicine has highlighted the importance of opening up overseas centers. Some of the Ayurvedic centers of Kerala have opened overseas centers resulting in the creation of overseas employment opportunities. A negative impact of the growth of *Ayurveda* in the West is their tendency to simplify *Ayurveda,* which is a skilled method of healing as some massages along with Indian music. The new interest in *Ayurveda* is due to the result of shifting

patterns in the western countries where people are more interested in alternative lifestyles and cultures.

There is an experimental proof that thirty percent of tourists to Kerala are for health holidays. This will help real estate, hospitality, transport and food & beverage industries. Ayurvedic tourism development has helped skilled, semi-skilled and non-skilled people in gaining employment even in other allied industries too. Ayurvedic tourism has enriched the wide range of attractions of Kerala helping it regain its position as a land of different types of attractions. Diversification of tourism products has resulted in repeated visits too. The study revealed that 90% of the customers in approved Ayurveda centers are from foreign countries. Generally in tourism industry, a significant part of the earnings will be spend for improving goods meant for tourists. As a result, the benefit will leak away. Since Ayurveda is using traditional resources, practices and facilities, the earnings will remain in the society.

84.2 percent of international tourists are attracted to Ayurvedic treatments through websites. This shows the significance of adoption of modern communication means for effective marketing. As marketing tools websites are followed by information through word of mouth and brochures. Since Ayurvedic health holidays are in the growth stage, more effective focused marketing techniques targeting the potential customers are required to attract more tourists. Majority of tourists visited Ayurvedic centers for rejuvenation of their mind and body. The increased health consciousness and the lack of fear on side effects is the major reason. The repeated visits to government approved Ayurvedic centers shows the quality and efficacy of treatments offered there. When compared to Ayurvedic spas in hotels the Ayurvedic resorts gained less tourists but the duration of treatments are high as these resorts are offering complete Ayurvedic treatments. Ayurvedic spas associated with hotels offers treatment of shorter

duration and attract more customers than Ayurvedic resorts. Out of 33 approved Ayurvedic centers in Kerala, the majority are situated in Southern Kerala. Although Ayurvedic hospitals, Ayurvedic resorts and hotels are offering Ayurvedic treatments, more treatment centers with good facilities are required as the number of tourists is increasing. The need of the hour is Ayurvedic centers with excellent standards. More centers assuring cleanliness and quality of treatments are required for increasing future tourist arrivals. Study at prominent tourist destinations revealed that the average duration of stay of foreign tourist in Kerala is 14.1 days. One of the major reasons behind this long duration of stay is the Ayurvedic treatments which has longer treatment duration.

Ayurvedic tourism development has helped protection of Kerala's architecture too. Many of the old houses and mansions constructed in Kerala style i.e., the *"Nalukettu"* and *"Ettukettu"* were refurnished to start Ayurvedic centers. Many of these damaged houses were dismantled and carefully reconstructed at tourist destinations.

The tourists who are attracted Ayurvedic centers are explorers and whose main interest is to experience and understand the Indian system of medicine and practices. Majority of the tourists belonged to this group and understands the richness and uniqueness of Indian way of life and adapts fully with the circumstances. This resulted in reducing the scope for host-guest encounters. Health tourism has benefited the Kerala society in the form of increased communication with other people, improved self image of Kerala society in other countries, growing range of employment opportunities, motivation for learning, modernization of infrastructure and increased urbanization.

The study revealed that Ayurvedic centers are offering *Panchakarma* treatment and its pre-operative and post-operative treatments. The science of *Ayurveda* is much beyond *Panchakarma* which includes the elaborate eight branches of the Vedic science. The emergence of this new

area of activity has helped the small state of Kerala in gaining much in monetary terms. Although it had a tremendous scope for development, the inadequate quality of services and facilities are major hindrances for its sustainability.

6.2 Major Suggestions

1. To develop the Ayurvedic tourism market further, marketing campaign shall be done among Indian communities, especially Non resident Keralites who are familiarized with *Ayurveda,* to increase tourist arrivals during monsoon.
2. The hotels who offer short term massages and peripheral applications, should call themselves 'well being centers' and not 'Ayurvedic centers'.
3. Direct flights to Kerala from the major tourist generating countries of Western Europe, United States of America and Australia can help further growth of tourist arrivals.
4. The heavy taxes charged by the state government of Kerala on hotel rooms, and food and liquor meant for tourists shall be reduced to a reasonable level.
5. Medicinal Plants Board shall be strengthened to promote cultivation of various medicinal plants keeping in mind the external and internal demands. Central and state government assistance for the owners of medicinal gardens shall be routed through this board only.
6. The state government should constitute a Tourism Promotion Council with non-resident Keralites. The major migrant workforce of Kerala origin in other countries shall be given a role in tourism promotion of Kerala.
7. Ayurvedic centers shall be categorized into three,

and price of Ayurvedic treatments shall be fixed based on the facilities there.

8. Clinical laboratories shall be opened along with Ayurvedic centers to test blood, urine etc.
9. Working time shall be fixed for all institutions offering Ayurvedic treatment facilities to tourists.
10. The government should frame rules to ban Ayurvedic centers running without doctors and without treatment facilities. The approval and classification scheme shall be made compulsory to all centers offering treatment facilities to tourists.
11. Toilets of global standards shall be constructed at all tourist destinations.
12. The government should entrust local bodies to function as watchdogs for ensuring high quality of service at Ayurvedic centers.
13. A mechanism to monitor the quality of herbal products and medicines shall evolve. Measures for periodic banning of substandard batches of Ayurvedic medicines shall be taken.
14. Legal measures shall be taken to curtail practice of depicting dietary supplements as medicines.
15. Drug manufacturing companies shall be asked to mention the names of ingredients on drug bottles and packets.
16. Ayurvedic educational institutions and courses have to be upgraded to incorporate break through in research and technology.
17. Measures shall be taken to invest in research and development. Clinical analysis of popular medicines and scientific confirmations can create global attention on Ayurvedic products.
18. *Ayurveda* has to be integrated with other mainstream

systems of medicine to bring up the idea of integrated medicine and to meet the health requirements of people. This is due to the failure of any single system of medicine to fully satisfy human community's growing health requirements. Holistic villages offering all such facilities shall be formed.

19. *Ayurveda* can be linked up with other attractions like folk arts of North Kerala or its heritage spots. The art forms like *theyyam* and *thira* will enrich the total tourism experience.
20. Collection, cataloguing and digitalization of ancient Ayurvedic manuscripts are required.
21. Marketing of tourism products abroad shall take into consideration the number of popular Indian restaurants. Marketing strategies focused on these restaurants situated at prominent cities of the world will give more results, than marketing focused on a wider society.
22. Facilities for blind, infirm and handicapped visitors shall be arranged at various centers. This shall be given high priority during resort and accommodation planning.
23. The Kerala example of Ayurvedic health holidays can be followed by states like Uttarakhand, Himachal Pradesh etc. which are famous for their Ayurvedic tradition and presence of precious herbs.

6.3 Scope for Further Study

The scope for further studies in tourism is given below;

1. Comparative study of Ayurvedic tourism and other rejuvenating health therapies of the world.
2. Carrying capacities of various tourism areas which gives thrust to new resources in tourism.

3. The involvement of ethnic factors in the development of tourism in Kerala.
4. Importance of information technology in marketing tourism.
5. Environmental impact of back water holidays may be studied.
6. Universities should form independent departments in tourism and travel management giving thrust to research activities in tourism along with running degree and post graduate courses in tourism.

6.4 Conclusion

Kerala, the southern state of India, has been referred as a paradise for tourists by the media world wide. A gradual growth in both foreign and domestic tourist arrivals has happened in the last decade. This is mainly due to the diversification and enrichment of existing tourism products, by adding more products like Ayurvedic health holidays, back water holidays, eco tourism etc. The study has revealed the plight of Ayurvedic tourism in Kerala. A number of measures are to be taken to sustain the growth of Ayurvedic holidays. The study has also noted the problems faced by the Ayurvedic tourism industry. An attempt has been made to study the socio-economic impacts of Ayurvedic tourism. The tourism planners, entrepreneurs and policy makers should carefully address the problems faced by this growing industry. Opening up of Ayurveda cautiously and systematically will result in the all round economic development of Kerala.

Bibliography

Government Reports and Orders

Tourist Statistics 1986–2000—Department of Tourism, Government of Kerala.

Tourist Profile Survey—Department of Tourism, Government of Kerala.

Tourism Policy of Kerala—Department of Tourism, Government of Kerala, 1995.

Draft Tourism Vision 2025—Department of Tourism, Government of Kerala.

Government order no. (MS) No. 140/98/GAD, 23 March 1998.

Government order no. (MS) No. 331/98/GAD, 28 April 1998.

Government order no. (MS) No. 35/2002/GAD, 28 January 2002.

Books

Bhatia, A.K. (1994); *International Tourism: Fundamentals and Practices,* Sterling Publishers, New Delhi.

Chattopadhyay, Kunal (1995); *Economic Impact of Tourism Development—An Indian Experience,* Kanishka Publishers, New Delhi.

Chopra, Sunita (1991); *Tourism and Development in India,* Ashish Publishing House, New Delhi.

Compendium of Invited Lectures (2002); World Ayurveda Congress, Kochi.

Cook, Roy A, Yale, Laura, Marqua, Joseph (1999); *Tourism—The Business of Travel,* Prentice Hall, New Jersey.

Cooper, Chris (1994); *Tourism—Principles and Practice,* Pitman Publishing, London.

Dahanukar, Sharadini & Thatte, Urmila (2000); *Ayurveda Revisited,* Popular Prakashan, Bombay.

Davidson, Rob (1994); *Tourism,* Pitman Publishers, London.

Fay, Betsy (1996); *Essentials of Tour Management,* Prentice Hall, New Jersey.

Garg, Nirmalkumar (1996); *Tourism and Economic Development,* APH Publishers, New Delhi.

Ghosh, Bishwanath (2000); *Tourism and Travel Management,* Vikas Publishing House, New Delhi.

Gill, Pushpinder (1997); *Dynamics of Tourism*—volume 3, Anmol Publications, New Delhi.

Hollway, Christopher (1994); *The Business of Tourism,* Pitman Publishing, London.

Jagannathan, Shakunthala (1994); *Plan your own Holiday,* Vakils Feffer and Simons Ltd., Bombay.

Joshy, Sunil V. (1997); *Ayurveda and Panchakarma,* Motilal Banarsidass Publishers, Delhi.

Kotler, Philip (1995); *Marketing Management: Analysis, Planning, Implementation and Control*, Prentice Hall, New Delhi.

Kotler, Philip (1995); *Principles of Marketing*, Prentice Hall, New Delhi.

Kotler, Philip, Bowen, John & Makens, James (1997); *Marketing for Hospitality and Tourism*, Prentice Hall, London.

Kumar, Ravibhushan (1995); *Coastal Tourism and Environment*, APH publishing Corporation, New Delhi.

Lea, John (1995); *Tourism in Third World Countries*, Routledge, London.

Medlik, S. and Bukart (1998); *Tourism: Past, Present and Future*, Heinemann, London.

Menon, K.M. (1999); *Tourism Management in India*, Printwell Publishers, Jaipur;.

Menon, Sreedhara A. (1996); *A Survey of Kerala History*, S. Viswanathan Pvt. Ltd., Madras.

Menon, Sreedhara A. (1990); *Kerala History and its Makers*, S. Viswanathan Pvt. Ltd., Madras.

Middleton, Victor T.C. (1994); *Marketing in Travel and Tourism*, Oxford, Butterworth Heinemann.

Mill, R.C. & Morrison (1998); *The Tourism System: An Introductory Text*, Prentice Hall, New Jersey.

Mill, R.C. (2001); *Resorts: Management and Opèration*, John Wiley & Sons, New York.

Murthy, N.A. & Pandey (2000); *Ayurvedic Cure for Common Diseases*, Orient Paperbacks, New Delhi.

Nair, Ramachandran S. (1999); *Social and Cultural History of Colonial Ernakulam*, Nalanda Books, Kerala.

Oomman, Priyan C. (1995); *Tourism Directory of Kerala*, Global Communications, Trivandrum.

Ritchie, Brent J.R. & Goeldner, Charles R. (1994); *Travel, Tourism and Hospitality Research*, John Wiley & Sons, New York.

Sajnani, Manohar (1989); *Tourism Business—A Legal Perspective*, Gyan Publishing House, New Delhi.

Sarkar, Arunkumar & Dhar, Premnath (1998); *Indian Tourism—Economic Planning and Strategies*, Kanishka Publications, New Delhi.

Sengupta, Kaviraj N.N. (1995); *Ayurvedic System of Medicine 2 volumes*, CBH Publications, Nagercoil.

Sinha, P.C. (1997); *International Encyclopedia of Tourism Management*—Volume eight, Anmol Publications, New Delhi.

Souvenir (2002); *World Ayurveda Congress*, Kochi.

Starr, Nona (2000); *View Point—An Introduction to Travel, Tourism and Hospitality*, Prentice Hall, New Jersey.

Sudheer, S.V. (1993); *Tourism—Problems and Prospects*, CBH Publications, Trivandrum,

Svoboda, Robert & Lade, Arnie (1980); *Chinese Medicine and Ayurveda*, Motilal Banarsidass Publishers, Delhi.

Trivedi, Priya Ranjan (1994); *International encyclopaedia of Ecology and Environment*, Indian Institute of Ecology and Environment, New Delhi

Varrier, Krishna P.K. and Sharma, Subramanya S. (1982); *Keraleeyachikitsa*, Vasudeva Vilasom Pharmacy, Thiruvananthapuram.

Warrier, Krishnankutty—*Ayurveda Charitram* (Malayalam).

Webster, Susan (1993); *Group Travel Operating Procedures*, Van Nostrand Reinhold, New York.

World Tourism Organisation (1995); *National and Regional Tourism Planning*, Routledge, London.

Consulted News Papers and Periodicals

The Indian Express (Calicut)

The Hindu (Coimbatore)

The Business Times

Malayala Manorama (Calicut)

Mathrubhoomi (Calicut)

Science India (Thirvananthapuram)

Mathrubhoomi Arogyamasika (Malayalam, Calicut)

Select List of Tourism Brochures

Ayurveda—Harmony of body, mind and soul, Sree Sankara Community for Ayurveda consciousness Ltd., Changanacherry, Kerala.

Ayurvedic Health Holidays in Kerala, Department of Tourism, Kerala, Thiruvananthapuram.

Backwaters, Department of Tourism, Kerala, Thiruvananthapuram.

Classification scheme for Ayurveda centers, Department of Tourism, Kerala, Thiruvananthapuram.

Fairs and Festivals of Kerala—Department of Tourism, Kerala, Thiruvananthapuram.

Festive Kerala, Department of Tourism, Kerala, Thiruvananthapuram.

Heavenly Hideaways in God's own Country, K.T.D.C Thiruvananthapuram.

Kerala—India's Natural Park, Tourist Desk, Cochin.

Kerala Beckons, Department of Tourism, Kerala, Thiruvananthapuram.

Make Tourism Your Business Too, Department of Tourism, *Kerala,*. Thiruvananthapuram.

Monsoon Rejuvenation Holidays, Department of Tourism, *Kerala,* Thiruvananthapuram.

Spreading the spirit of tourism, Department of Tourism, Kerala, Thiruvananthapuram.

The Essential Kerala, Department of Tourism, Kerala, Thiruvananthapuram.

The Great Kerala Getaways, Department of Tourism, Kerala, Thiruvananthapuram.

The Kerala Companion, Department of Tourism, Kerala, Thiruvananthapuram.

Tourist's Map of Kerala, Department of Tourism, Kerala, Thiruvananthapuram.

Your Health: Our concern, KAPL Ayurclinic, Kerala Ayurveda Pharmacy Ltd., Thiruvananthapuram.

Index